Pegan Diet Cookbook for Beginners

100 Simple and Delicious Recipes with Pictures to Easily Add Healthy Meals to Your Busy Schedule

By: Nathalie Seaton

TABLE OF CONTENTS

INTRODUCTION 7

CHAPTER 1: MUST-KNOW CONCEPTS OF A VEGAN DIET 11
- What Is the Vegan Diet? 11
- The Different Types of Vegan Diet 13
- The Basic Guidelines of Veganism 14
- Allowed Foods 14
- Restricted Foods 15

CHAPTER 2: MUST-KNOW CONCEPTS OF A PALEO DIET 17
- Having a Look at What the Cave-Dwellers Ate 17
- Amazing Advantages of Following This Diet 18
- The Paleo Food List 20
- A Note on Drinking 28

CHAPTER 3: PEGAN DIET – THE BEST OF BOTH WORLDS 30
- What Is the Pegan Diet? 30
- The Main Idea of a Pegan Diet 32
- The Combined Health Benefits of the Pegan Diet 36

CHAPTER 4: THE PEGAN DIET STARTER GUIDE 42
- You Should Plan for Success 42
- Setting Up Your Pegan Pantry 43
- Setting Up Your Pegan Kitchen 48
- A Note on Choosing Your Containers 50
- The 14-Day Meal Plan 53
- What to Expect After 14 Days 55
- A Note on Dining Out, Pegan Style 55

CHAPTER 5: THE MEAL PLANNING GUIDE 57
- What Exactly is Meal Prep? 57
- The Advantages of Meal Prep 57
- The Very Basics of Meal Prep 58
  - *Step 1: Choose a Day* 58
  - *Step 2: Choose Your Meals* 59
  - *Step 3: Equipment and Shopping List* 59
  - *Step 4: The Process* 60

CHAPTER 6: BREAKFAST AND BRUNCH RECIPES ... 64
1. Awesome Overnight Chia Pudding (Vegan) ... 64
2. Healthy Pancakes With Berry Syrup (Vegetarian) ... 66
3. Lovely Avocado Baked-Eggs (Vegetarian | Low-Carb) ... 68
4. Healthy Nut Porridge (Vegan) ... 70
5. Flaxseed Porridge (Vegan | Low-Carb) ... 72
6. Cool Green Smoothie (Vegan) ... 74
7. Chilled Cinnamon Smoothie (Vegan | Low-Carb) ... 75
8. Peanut Butter and Cocoa Smoothie (Vegan | Low-Carb) ... 76
9. Excellent No-Bake Breakfast Cookies (Vegan | Low-Carb) ... 78
10. Morning Strawberry Chia Jam (Vegan | Low-Carb) ... 80
11. Healthy Raspberry Smoothie (Vegan) ... 82
12. Chia and Flax Porridge (Vegan) ... 84
13. Vanilla Hemp Drink (Vegan) ... 86
14. Macadamia Protein Smoothie (Vegan | Low-Carb) ... 88
15. Coconut and Hazelnut Chiller (Vegan) ... 89
16. Flavorful Breakfast Hash (Vegan) ... 90
17. Awesome Strawberry Shake (Vegetarian) ... 92
18. Cinnamon and Coconut Porridge (Vegetarian | Low-Carb) ... 94

CHAPTER 7: PLANT-BASED MAINS ... 96
19. Green Beans and Onion Roast (Vegan | Low-Carb) ... 96
20. Cauliflower and Mushroom Risotto (Vegan) ... 98
21. Brussels Lemon Delight (Vegan | Low-Carb) ... 100
22. Skillet Kale and Avocado (Vegetarian | Low-Carb) ... 102
23. Almond and Blistered Beans (Vegan | Low-Carb) ... 104

CHAPTER 8: VEGETARIAN SOUPS, SALADS, AND SNACKS ... 106
24. Coconut and Cauliflower Rice Delight (Vegan | Low-Carb) ... 106
25. Awesome Garlic and Kale (Vegan | Low-Carb) ... 108
26. BBQ'd Zucchini Delight (Vegan | Low-Carb) ... 110
27. Perfect Cucumber-Tomato Gazpacho (Vegan) ... 112
28. Cool Healthy Guacamole (Vegan) ... 114
29. Hearty Tomato Platter (Vegetarian) ... 116
30. Lovely Tomato Salad (Low-Carb | Vegan) ... 118
31. Perfect Veggie Packed Soup (Low-Carb | Vegan) ... 120
32. Creamy Mushroom Soup (Vegan | Low-Carb) ... 122
33. Awesome Kale and Spinach Bowl (Vegan | Low-Carb) ... 124
34. Roasted Garlic Soup (Vegan | Low-Carb) ... 126
35. The Perfect Zucchini Bowl (Low-Carb | Vegan) ... 128

36. ASPARAGUS AND WALNUTS SAUTÉ (LOW-CARB | VEGAN) 130

CHAPTER 9: CHICKEN AND POULTRY **132**

    37. ALMOND BREADED CHICKEN (LOW-CARB) 132
    38. BLACKBERRY CHICKEN WINGS (LOW-CARB) 134
    39. LETTUCE TURKEY WRAP (LOW-CARB) 136
    40. CHICKEN DINNER CASSEROLE (LOW-CARB) 138
    41. CHICKEN AND BASIL WITH ZUCCHINI ZOODLES 140
    42. BLACKENED CHICKEN (LOW-CARB) 142
    43. STIR-FRIED CHICKEN CHOW-MEIN (LOW-CARB) 144
    44. SIMPLE PARSLEY CHICKEN BREAST (LOW-CARB) 146
    45. SPICY CHIPOTLE LETTUCE CHICKEN 148
    46. JUICY MUSTARD CHICKEN 150
    47. BUFFALO LETTUCE WRAPS (LOW-CARB) 152
    48. ITALIAN HERBED BALSAMIC CHICKEN (LOW-CARB) 154
    49. GREEK CHICKEN BREAST (LOW-CARB) 156
    50. EASY STIR-FRIED CHICKEN 158
    51. SPINACH CHICKEN BREAST SALAD (LOW-CARB) 160

CHAPTER 10: BEEF RECIPES **162**

    52. ASIAN BEEF STEAK (LOW-CARB) 162
    53. AVOCADO BEEF PATTIES 164
    54. FRESH THAI BEEF DISH (LOW-CARB) 166
    55. BEEF ZUCCHINI HALVES (LOW-CARB) 168
    56. BEEF AND TOMATO SQUASH (LOW-CARB) 170
    57. JUICY BEEF STUFFED BELL PEPPER (LOW-CARB) 172
    58. TAMARI STEAK SALAD (LOW-CARB) 174
    59. ZUCCHINI AND BEEF SAUTÉ (LOW-CARB) 176
    60. CABBAGE FRIED BEEF (LOW-CARB) 178
    61. MUSHROOM AND MEDITERRANEAN STEAK 180
    62. BEEF POT ROAST (LOW-CARB) 182
    63. STIR-FRIED GROUND BEEF (LOW-CARB) 184
    64. PEPPER BEEF STEAK STIR FRY (LOW-CARB) 186
    65. VEGETABLE AND BEEF STEAK WITH CHIMICHURRI (LOW-CARB) 188

CHAPTER 11: PORK AND OTHER RED MEATS **190**

    66. CLASSICAL MEDITERRANEAN PORK (LOW-CARB) 190
    67. BACON AND ONION PORK CHOPS (LOW-CARB) 192
    68. PORK STUFFED BELL PEPPERS (LOW-CARB) 194
    69. CARAMELIZED PORK CHOPS (LOW-CARB) 196

70. Italian Pork Chops (Low-Carb) 198
71. Mushroom Pork Chops (Low-Carb) 200
72. Paprika Lamb Chops (Low-Carb) 202
73. Fennel and Figs Lamb (Low-Carb) 204
74. Hearty Lamb Salad (Low-Carb) 206
75. Simple Lamb Chops (Low-Carb) 208
76. South Western Pork Chops (Low-Carb) 210
77. Smothered Pork Chops (Low-Carb) 212
78. Skillet Baked Pork Chops and Apple 214
79. Sesame Pork Chops (Low-Carb) 216
80. Stir Fry Pork 218
81. Spicy Pork Chop (Low-Carb) 220

CHAPTER 12: FISH AND SEAFOOD 222

82. Walnut Encrusted Salmon (Low-Carb) 222
83. Awesome Glazed Salmon (Low-Carb) 224
84. Baked Orange Juice Salmon (Low-Carb) 226
85. Broccoli and Tilapia Dish (Low-Carb) 228
86. Baked Halibut 230
87. Garlic and Parsley Scallops (Low-Carb) 232
88. Coconut and Hazelnut Haddock (Low-Carb) 234
89. Italian Salmon Platter (Low-Carb) 236
90. Feisty Grilled Lime Shrimp (Low-Carb) 238
91. Exciting Calamari 240

CHAPTER 13: SNACKS AND APPETIZERS 242

92. Cool Warm Green Beans Dish (Low-Carb | Vegan) 242
93. Lemon Broccoli Roast (Low-Carb | Vegan) 244
94. Cool Avocado Chips (Low-Carb | Vegan) 246
95. Exotic Cucumber Sushi (Low-Carb | Vegan) 248
96. Roasted Herb Crackers (Low-Carb | Vegan) 250
97. Onion and Thyme Crackers (Low-Carb | Vegan) 252
98. Awesome Cacao Nut Truffles 254
99. Walnuts and Asparagus Combo (Low-Carb | Vegan) 256
100. Garlic Lemon Soup (Low-Carb | Vegan) 258
101. Pumpkin Spicy Chili Dish 260

CONCLUSION 263

SPECIAL BONUS!

Want This Bonus book for FREE?

Get **FREE** unlimited access to it and all of my new books by joining the Fan Base!

SCAN W/ YOUR CAMERA TO JOIN!

Introduction

Despite being extremely popular these days, the Pegan diet is still somewhat of a mystery to people who are just beginning to scratch the surface of this absolutely incredible diet plan. And the confusion always seems to stem from the name of the diet itself!

"PEGAN"

The name does sound pretty confusing, doesn't it? Well, it's really not. Some people might tell you that the Pegan Diet is very similar to that of a Keto Diet—however, that is not entirely true. The Pegan Diet does have some similarity to the Keto Diet, but it is not as restrictive in terms of carb or macronutrient counts. That being said, though, there are many recipes present here that can be used when following the more restrictive Keto Diet routine.

Keep in mind that many of the recipes are also marked with a notation that tells whether the recipes are suitable for specific lifestyles like Vegan, Vegetarian, or Low-Carb. I do believe that this will help you to quickly find the most desirable recipes for your menu plan.

The Pegan Diet is essentially a method that seamlessly blends the well-known Paleo Diet principles with those of the Vegan diet and fuses them into what is known as the Pegan Diet. Dr. Mark Hyman was the first individual to coin this term—on his blog back in 2014. However, it wasn't until recently that the diet started to gather steam and soar in popularity.

For those of you who don't recognize the name, Dr. Mark Hyman is a leading figure in the world of health and medical sciences. He revolutionized the concept of using food to support various lifestyle factors such as longevity, mental clarity, energy, happiness, and more. Dr. Hyman is a private physician as well as a globally recognized and decorated leader, speaker, educator, and outstanding advocate in the field of medicine.

He also stands as the founder and director of the UltraWellness Center, and he's the head of Strategy and Innovation at the Cleveland Clinic Center for Functional Medicine.

Throughout his long-running career, he had the privilege of collaborating with several high-level celebrities and notable figures—working extensively on books, health routines, and so on.

He worked with Rick Warren, Dr. Mehmet Oz, and Dr. Daniel Amen on a book called *The Daniel Plan*, which won the Christian book of the year award. He had the esteemed privilege of being inducted into the Books for Better Life hall of fame with Dr. Dean Ornish. He collaborated with Tim Ryan to introduce the "ENRICH" Act into Congress in hopes of funding nutrition in medical education, and he gave various health advice to none other than former President Bill Clinton after his quadruple bypass surgery.

So, as you can already tell, Dr. Hyman is a man with a large pedigree of success behind him, and his credibility in this field was one of the many reasons why I was so inspired to write a book based on his ideologies.

In fact, if statistics are to be believed, then according to Pinterest, the interest in this particular diet program has scaled up about 337% just last year, with searches not showing any sign of slowing down.

Being a simple wife, mother, and passionate writer, I am always trying to find the perfect balance between consuming good food and being healthy.

I am always searching for the most "Perfect Diet" while aware that nothing like that truly exists. However, all diets have their advantages, and I love to keep on exploring and sharing those ideas with my readers so they can easily digest and understand them. The more knowledge you have, the better decisions you will make when deciding which diet might be the best one for you.

During my exploratory journey, my attention was drawn to how Dr. Mark Hyman presented the ideas about his now incredible Pegan Diet. It promised to help a person reclaim their lost health and nutrition in a world where everything is so nutritionally confusing.

The Pegan diet tries its best to keep things as simple as possible, to ensure that its followers can enjoy all of the benefits without having to go through too much of a hassle.

In this book, I won't be attempting to re-invent the wheel and create new discoveries when it comes to Pegan Diet. Rather, my main aim here is to produce a beginner-friendly cookbook that covers the fundamentals of the Pegan diet while giving you a plethora of mouthwatering and absolutely delicious recipes to choose from.

The concept of combining a diet that focuses on consuming foods our ancestors ate with a Vegan diet might sound a bit restrictive. Still, the Pegan Diet is, in reality, far less restrictive than either of those diets on their own.

That's because the Pegan Diet mainly tries to take in both of those other diets' positive principles rather than their restrictions. This results in the Pegan Diet being very flexible, allowing for the consumption of some meat while limiting whole grains, legumes, and dairy.

Since this book is designed to be as beginner-friendly as possible, I tried to go as deep into the concepts as possible while keeping things simple.

The first two chapters of the book will cover the core concepts of the Paleo and Vegan Diets individually since Pegan is a combination of these two. I strongly believe that to fully appreciate what the Pegan Diet truly is, you need to understand its origins.

The third and fourth chapters focus strictly on the Pegan Diet, explaining the core idea and helping you to get into the diet— starting it off with a 14-day meal plan.

The fifth chapter is a bonus chapter that explains the core concepts of Meal Planning and teaches you how you can plan your meals ahead of time to make following the diet even easier.

And after that, Chapters 6-13 are packed to the brim with absolutely mouthwatering Pegan Diet-friendly recipes that are easy to make and are crafted with very simple and easy to source ingredients that you'll find at any of your local grocery stores.

So, what are you waiting for? Jump right in; welcome into the amazing Pegan world!

Chapter 1: Must-Know Concepts of a Vegan Diet

As mentioned in the introduction, since the Pegan Diet is essentially a combination of both the Vegan Diet and the Paleo Diet, I do believe that it is important that you have a good understanding of both of these diets on a separate level so that you can better understand the concepts of Pegan and appreciate it benefits even more.

That being said, we are first going to be walking through the Vegan Diet.

What Is the Vegan Diet?

In its simplest form, a vegan diet encourages an individual to follow a regime of food consumption that completely eliminates any kind of products or ingredients derived (directly or indirectly) from animals. This essentially means that meats are completely off the table, as well as animal-derived products such as cheese, milk, honey, etc.

As for the matter of "Why?" one should follow the vegan path, well...the opinion varies from person to person, to be honest.

The general consensus would tell you that people want to be vegan because they simply want to be "healthy." However, the individuals who take veganism directly to heart and follow it as a lifestyle would give you a different answer. For them, veganism isn't just a diet, but rather it is the definition of how they carve out their life. To them, it is nothing short of a peaceful revolution against animal cruelty and exploitation of the world.

Just in case you are wondering, it should be made clear that there is a fine difference between vegetarianism and veganism. Individuals who follow the Vegan Diet tend to completely restrict themselves from having any kind of dairy/animal products, as mentioned above. However, vegetarians have a certain level of freedom in this department, allowing them to have certain animal-derived products such as eggs or cheese.

The recipes in this book are based on the Vegan Diet; thus, the introductory chapter will also focus on veganism.

Now, let me introduce you to the different types of well-known vegan diets out there that you might consider taking up.

The Different Types of Vegan Diet

- **Whole Food Vegan Diet:** This diet basically emphasizes different kinds of whole plant foods such as nuts, seeds, legumes, fruits, whole grains, etc.
- **Raw-Food Vegan Diet:** This diet is composed of nuts, raw fruits, plant foods, vegetables, and seeds cooked under 118 degrees Fahrenheit.
- **80/10/10:** This special diet encourages an individual to rely on fat-rich plants such as avocados and nuts and focuses more on raw fruits and tender greens. This diet is also known as the "Fruitarian Diet."
- **The Starch Solution:** This is similar to the above Fruitarian Diet except that it focuses on cooked starches such as rice, potatoes, and corn instead of raw fruits.
- **Raw Till 4:** This is a low-fat diet that is a variation of the Fruitarian and Starch Solution diet. In this diet, raw fruits are consumed up until 4 PM, after which the individual can cook a nice plant-based meal to end the day.
- **Junk Food Vegan Diet:** This diet relies largely on mock meats and vegan-compliant cheese, desserts, and fries—not to mention other heavily processed vegan products as well!

The different forms of the diet allow each individual to pick the one that best suits their lifestyle. The diet's versatility also allows certain individuals who might be suffering from any kind of health condition to pick a form of vegan diet to best suit their needs.

The Basic Guidelines of Veganism

Don't be alarmed by the different types of diet, though! Suppose you want to avoid all the confusing aspects of the diet and simply embark on a vegan diet's most generic form. In that case, all you have to do is follow the basic guidelines of the diet.

- Try to eat at least five portions of veggies and fruits per day, with loads of variety.
- Make sure to keep your base meals centered around rice, bread, potatoes, pasta, and other starchy carbs.
- Go for dairy alternatives such as soya drinks, yogurt, and other low fat/low sugar options.
- Try to pack in some pulses and beans to ensure that you are supplied with protein.
- If using oils and spreads, make sure to go for unsaturated ones and use these in small portions.
- Make sure to keep yourself packed with lots of fluids—preferably 6-8 cups per day.

Allowed Foods

These are the foods that should always be on your list.

- **Tofu, Seitan, and Tempeh:** These are excellent sources of protein and are rich alternatives to fish, poultry, and meat.
- **Legumes:** These include beans, peas, and lentils, which are also great sources of many essential nutrients and beneficial plant compounds.
- **Nuts and Nut Butters:** Go for pure unroasted and unblanched ones, as these are packed with selenium, zinc, fiber, iron, etc.

- **Seeds:** Flaxseed, hemp, and chia are good choices for seeds, as they are packed with a good dose of omega-3 fatty acids and protein.
- **Algae:** Chlorella and Spirulina are good choices for seeking out good sources of protein-packed algae.
- **Calcium Fortified Plant Milks and Yogurts:** These are excellent alternatives for a vegan to meet their daily recommended dietary calcium intake.
- **Nutritional Yeast:** This is yet another means of easily obtaining a large amount of protein from vegan meals. Make sure to go for yeast that is labeled "Vitamin B12 fortified" for maximum benefit.
- **Sprouted and Fermented Plant Foods:** Produce such as tempeh, natto, miso, pickles, kombucha, and Kimchi fall under this category; they offer a good amount of vitamin K2 and probiotics.
- **Whole Grain Cereals and Pseudocereals:** These are good providers of complex carbs, iron, and Vitamin B.

And, of course...

- **Vegetables and Fruits:** These should make up the bulk of your diet. They are excellent sources of nutrients, and leafy greens such as bok choy, kale, mustard greens, and even spinaches are jam-packed with calcium and iron.

Restricted Foods

These are the items that are avoided at all costs.

- **Meat:** Lamb, beef, horse, veal, organ meat, chicken, wild meat, goose, turkey, quail, duck, etc.
- **Fish and Seafood:** All types of seafood are restricted, including squid, shrimp, anchovies, calamari, crab, etc.

- **Eggs:** Any kind of eggs, including ostrich, quail, chicken, and fish, are off the table.
- **Dairy:** Ice Cream, cheese, cream, milk, butter are restricted.
- **Animal-Based Products and Ingredients:** whey, lactose, casein, egg white albumen, carmine, gelatin, etc., are to be avoided.
- **Bee Products:** royal jelly, pollen, honey, etc., are to be avoided.

Chapter 2: Must-Know Concepts of a Paleo Diet

The Paleo Diet's core objective harkens back to the glorious days of the cave-dwellers and re-orients our dietary regime, emphasizing more on what these ancestors ate.

That was a time, way before the agricultural revolution, when people relied mostly on simple foods that were available to them through foraging or hunting.

This essentially meant that foods and ingredients that were naturally available, such as fruits, vegetables, berries, meat, etc., were on the table, while any type of processed food was not.

This is what lies at the heart of the Paleo Diet.

Having a Look at What the Cave-Dwellers Ate

In the previous section, you may have noticed that I used the word "cave-dweller" to describe followers of the original Paleo Diet.

Let me go into a bit more depth here.

Whenever we talk about a cave-dweller's diet, we are mostly referring to a diet that can offer us the right amount of protein, calories, carbs, etc., without overly relying on processed or toxic foods.

Generally speaking, research from Emory University suggests that it is advisable for people who follow a paleo diet to take 35% of their total calorie intake from fats, 35% from carbohydrates, and the final 30% from proteins.

Amazing Advantages of Following This Diet

The Paleo Diet comes with a barrage of fantastic health benefits that you will enjoy in the long run!

To encourage you to explore the diet itself even further and embrace its way of life, here are just some of the crucial advantages!

Accelerated Weight Loss

The low-carb, clean-eating regime of the Paleo Diet dramatically helps to turn the body into a fat-burning machine that accelerates the amount of fat used up by various activities.

This is discussed in greater detail in a section later on.

Improved Intestinal Health

A diet consisting of highly processed foods and chemicals often leads to stomach and intestinal lining issues and causes leaky gut and other problems. Since the Paleo Diet encourages you to let go of all of these harmful food items, you will eventually start to protect your gut's health and improve any problems you already have.

Provides the Right Amount of Vitamins and Minerals

The traditional Western diet that we usually tend to follow contains more rubbish and less nutrition! The Paleo Diet will help you bring a sense of balance into the food you consume and provide you with sufficient minerals and vitamins to keep you healthy.

Eliminates Allergens From the Diet

The food list of the Paleo Diet is designed to greatly reduce allergens such as dairy and grains from the diet, improving your overall tolerance in the long run.

Lowers Inflammation

A paleo diet encourages an individual to choose foods rich in Omega-3 fatty acids, and these foods have been shown to reduce inflammation.

The benefit? With reduced inflammation, you will start to experience relief from various autoimmune diseases such as rheumatoid arthritis, bronchitis, sinusitis, asthma, etc.

The Paleo Diet has also been known to improve your cardiovascular health as well!

Gives More Energy

A clean and healthy diet plan will allow your body to have more energy to spend naturally!

Unlike processed foods, the healthy alternatives will stay in your body for a long time and slowly keep releasing energy throughout the day.

This allows your body to stay pumped and avoids any feeling of lethargy!

And this is just the tip of the iceberg!

The Paleo Food List

You must be wondering about which foods are allowed on the Paleo Diet. Well, to give you a rough summary...

Foods to eat

- Meats, including lamb, beef, turkey, chicken, and pork
- Seafood, such as trout, haddock, and shellfish
- Eggs
- Lots and lots of vegetables, including peppers, kale, broccoli, carrots, onions, etc.
- Fruits such as bananas, apples, pears, strawberries, avocados, and blueberries
- Tubers, including sweet potatoes, turnips, and yams
- Nuts and seeds, such as macadamia, almonds, walnuts, hazelnuts, and sunflower seeds
- Fats and oils, such as coconut oil, avocado oil, and olive oil
- Salts such as Himalayan Salt, sea salt, turmeric, garlic, and rosemary

Foods not to eat

- Items that are high in fructose or sugar such as drinks, candy, and fruit juices
- Grain-type items such as wheat, rye, and barley
- Legumes, such as lentils
- Vegetable oils, such as corn oil, sunflower oil, and soybean oil
- Hydrogenated products
- Artificial sweeteners
- Heavily processed foods

And now, let me dive a little bit deeper into the allowed list.

Meat

The following is a list of meats that you can enjoy while on a paleo diet. Remember to try to obtain them as fresh as possible and avoid processed meats such as hot dogs, Spam, etc.

- Chicken liver
- Pork loin
- Duck
- Goat meat
- Lean hamburger
- Chuck steak
- Lean beef
- Flank steak
- Lean chicken breast
- Pork chops
- Turkey breast
- Goose
- Lean poultry
- Lean pork, trimmed
- Top sirloin steak
- Lean veal
- Rabbit meat
- Organ meats of chicken, beef, pork, and lamb

Fish and Seafood

Generally, all fish are allowed on a paleo diet as they are packed with omega-3 fatty acids.

- Scrod
- Shrimp
- Tuna
- Scallops

- Crab
- Herring
- Flatfish
- Red snapper
- Crayfish
- Lobster
- Monkfish
- Perch
- Halibut
- Mackerel
- Northern pike
- Trout
- Salmon
- Mussels
- Rockfish
- Turbot
- Drum
- Oysters
- Shark

Nuts and Seeds

When considering nuts, you should keep in mind that cashews are high in fat (and addictive!) so try to control your portions. If you are trying to lose weight while on a paleo diet, maybe you should consider cutting down your nut intake.

- Pecans
- Almonds
- Hazelnuts
- Walnuts
- Pumpkin seeds
- Sunflower seeds

- Brazil nuts
- Macadamia nuts
- Pistachios
- Cashews
- Sesame seeds
- Chestnuts
- Pine nuts

Veggies

Almost all veggies are allowed on a paleo diet! However, certain high-starch veggies such as squash and potatoes should be taken in moderation.

- Watercress
- Swiss chard
- Radish
- Turnips
- Asparagus
- Tomato
- Lettuce
- Bell peppers
- Turnip greens
- Kohlrabi
- Spinach
- Dandelion
- Seaweed
- Onions
- Parsnips
- Mustard greens
- Pumpkin
- Cauliflower
- Parsley

- Green onions
- Cabbage
- Mushrooms
- Kale
- Celery
- Mushrooms
- Broccoli
- Eggplant
- Collards
- Brussels sprouts
- Cucumber
- Artichokes
- Carrots
- Yam
- Acorn squash
- Butternut squash
- Beets
- Sweet potatoes

Oils and Fats

- Olive oil
- Coconut oil
- Avocado oil
- Macadamia oil

Fruits

Fruits are delicious and nutritious as well! Yet, they have a very high sugar value. Even the paleo-approved ones contain a hefty dose of fructose. Therefore, if your aim is to lose weight, try to keep your fruit intake on a basal level and learn more about vegetables.

- Avocado
- Apple
- Blackberries
- Plums
- Peaches
- Papaya
- Grapes
- Mango
- Lychee
- Orange
- Lemon
- Lime
- Tangerine
- Cantaloupe
- Raspberries
- Strawberries
- Guava
- Watermelon
- Pineapple
- Bananas
- Figs

Spices and Herbs

- Cinnamon
- Caraway
- Bay leaves
- Anise
- Basil
- Celery seeds
- Cayenne pepper
- Ginger

- Garlic
- Chives
- Cilantro
- Coriander
- Clove
- Cumin
- Curry
- Dill
- Fenugreek
- Fennel
- Horseradish
- Juniper berry
- Lavender
- Lemongrass
- Rosemary
- Marjoram
- Wasabi
- Mint
- Vanilla
- Turmeric
- Tarragon
- Thyme
- Black Pepper
- Peppermint
- Parsley
- Paprika
- Oregano
- Mustard

And the foods to avoid...

As a general rule of thumb, you should avoid refined, processed foods as well as sugar, legumes, and grains. For a stricter paleo regime, you should avoid all dairy as well!

- Milk
- Yogurt
- Butter
- Kefir
- Buttermilk
- Cream
- Cottage cheese
- Dairy spreads
- Ice cream
- Soft drinks
- Fruit juices (canned). You can have fresh fruit juices from certain fruits such as orange, lemon, lime, pineapple, etc.
- Stay away from all sorts of grains
- Legumes
- Beans, including kidney beans, horse beans, fava beans, garbanzo beans, broad beans, black beans, white beans, red beans, pinto beans, navy beans, mung beans, lima beans, string beans, and green beans
- Peas, such as sugar snap peas, snow peas, chickpeas, black-eyed peas, lentils, miso, peanuts, peanut butter, soybeans, lupines, tofu, etc.
- All kinds of artificial sweeteners! (Use maple syrup or honey to sweeten food.)
- Salty/processed foods such as ketchup and French fries

A Note on Drinking

For those of you who like alcoholic beverages, the bad news is you ought to let go of them. However, here are some awesome alternatives that you might want to keep an eye out for.

Water

This is pretty self-explanatory! Water is the prime hydration of our body, and it satisfies our body's thirst like no other drink! Pure water is chemical and toxin-free and is the perfect drink for a paleo diet.

If plain water tastes a bit bland to you, you can always add a dash of lime to make things more interesting!

Herbal Teas

Using all types of natural teas made by steeping health-infused herbs in water is a great way to stay hydrated while on a paleo diet.

These natural fusions are excellent because they provide an outstanding balance between being delicious and being healthy.

Common herbals teas include ginger, peppermint, green tea, etc.

Fruit Juice

When considering fruit juices, always avoid the store-bought ones as they are usually packed to the brim with sugar and preservatives! Instead, opt for 100% natural juices that you extract yourself.

Keep in mind, though, that even naturally extracted fruit juices are packed with sugar, so try to drink them as seldom as possible.

Coffee and Tea

The Paleo Diet doesn't encourage caffeinated beverages, but if you find yourself in a tight spot, try to go for a cup of black tea or coffee without any added sugar.

Milk

Generally speaking, milk is prohibited in a paleo diet! However, you are still allowed to go for extremely minimal amounts of raw milk.

Alcohol

Most paleo diets support alcohol in very small moderations. Try to avoid them as much as possible!

Sodas/Diet Beverages

These are packed with chemicals and artificial flavorings and fall firmly on the negative side of the spectrum!

That's all that you need to know about the Paleo Diet.

In the next chapter, we will look at the Pegan Diet, which, as you can already tell by now, is a combination of both the Paleo Diet and the Vegan Diet, hence the name Pegan.

Chapter 3: Pegan Diet – The Best of Both Worlds

What Is the Pegan Diet?

At first glance, the name of the diet itself might seem a bit odd. Is it paleo? Is it vegan? Or is it something completely new? Well, let me clear up the confusion for you and explain the concept as clearly as possible.

For absolute newcomers, the Pegan Diet is essentially a fusion of both the Paleo Diet and the Vegan Diet, and it tries to combine the principles of both these diets so that you can enjoy the benefits of both worlds.

At first, it might seem a bit strange because in the Paleo Diet you are essentially required to consume simple food that was available in the paleolithic era millions of years ago—fruits, vegetables, nuts, fish, and meat—except for dairy, grains, sugar, and some legumes (Chapter 2 contains a detailed food list on this diet). The Vegan Diet, on the other hand and as you already know, focuses on the consumption of only plant-based foods and strictly avoids any sort of animal and animal-derived products.

When comparing these diets, it is pretty common for an individual to become confused, given that these methods contradict each other in more ways than one.

But the reality is that the Pegan Diet tries to combine certain elements and principles of both diets in a way that does not cause any contradiction. The general idea of the Pegan Diet is that you are supposed to consume nutrient-rich whole foods that can reduce inflammation, balance blood sugar, and bring the body back to optimal health.

Paleos and vegans themselves are pretty restrictive when it comes to diet; most people think that combining the two would result in a diet that is even more restrictive. But that's not the case at all! The Pegan Diet is actually much less restrictive than either Paleo or Vegan, as it tries to combine only the general principles and not the restrictions of those individual diets.

Much emphasis is placed on eating fruits and vegetables as in the Vegan Diet. Still, unlike the Vegan Diet, animal proteins such as meats and fish are allowed, as well as some nuts, seeds, and legumes. In fact, even some items that are banned by both are allowed here, such as oils and some processed sugars, but note that these should be highly restricted. The Pegan Diet is not a crash diet but rather a sustainable diet meant to be easy to stick with, allowing one to stay on it indefinitely rather than later on losing the willpower to continue.

The Main Idea of a Pegan Diet

Now that we have a basic idea of what makes up a proper Pegan diet, we should look at the principles or the tenets behind it. These are tenets that one has to be aware of, as it may be confusing to just use the rule of thumb. After all, a vegan diet is clear—one can eat only plant-based things. A paleo diet is also fairly clear; one should eat simple, unprocessed foods. However, as a Pegan diet is separate and less restrictive, the limitations and tenets are not as intuitive. To put it simply, the Pegan Diet's recommendations are basically sound: fresh, locally sourced, preferably organic food, nothing refined or processed, and a focus on not raising your blood sugar. Dr. Mark Hyman has stated that the Pegan Diet can be defined by one simple rule: **"If God made it, eat it; if man made it, leave it."**

Focus on having a mainly plant-based diet

The first tenet is that one should have a mostly plant-based diet. Though, as we stated earlier, the consumption of animal proteins is allowed, most of the things one eats should be plant-based. In fact, a good rule of thumb to go by is half or a bit more than half of one's plate should be filled with vegetables. About seven or eight cups of vegetables and fruits a day are the World Health Organization's recommendation. This would serve as a great starting point. However, not all plant-based foods should be eaten in great quantities. Some foods, such as starchy vegetables like potatoes and squash, should be limited. Most of the vegetable portion of a day's meals should be leafy greens instead. One aim of this diet is to help regulate one's blood sugar, meaning that prioritizing low-glycemic-index foods is important to the diet, and having foods high in simple carbohydrates—high-glycemic-index foods—would defeat the purpose.

Also, fruits should be limited according to the same principle behind limiting starchy vegetables. However, this tip is more for those who are overweight and have a greater need to manage their blood sugar. If one has no blood sugar problems, most fruit is fine. If one is plagued with low blood sugar, glycemic-index fruits should be chosen, with sweeter fruits being eaten every so often and treated more like candy than a regular part of one's dinner plate.

Make sure to consume healthy fats

The second tenet would be to aim at consuming healthy fats. Fats are a very important part of one's nutrition but remember that they are best consumed in their whole food form. Some of these better fats will be found in unprocessed foods such as nuts, seeds, avocados, and olive oil. Some animal products containing healthier fats would be eggs and some fatty fish, such as salmon, mackerel, herring, and sardines. Using extra virgin olive oil or avocado oil, or even coconut oil, to garnish uncooked dishes such as salads or to use in cooking, would help. Remember that this is not a vegan diet; animal and saturated fat from unprocessed sources is allowed, such as meats, fish, eggs, or even butter or ghee. Note, however, that saturated fat is very bad for you if it is combined with refined sugars and starches. Also, common oils such as vegetable, bean, and seed oils tend to be very processed. Thus, they are not recommended.

Consume meat in moderation

One of the most surprising things that people notice about the Pegan Diet is that it allows meat to be eaten, even if it takes a lot from the Vegan Diet. However, even if meat is allowed, it is recommended that it is kept to a small amount per meal. In fact, it should act as more of a side dish or condiment, with the vegetables making up the majority of the meal. Note that some forms of animal proteins other than poultry or grass-fed beef, such as insects, can be eaten. However, this may be for only the more adventurous souls.

Eat whole grains and beans

Make sure to include only whole grains in your diet and ignore other types of grains. In fact, even grain flours should be avoided. However, these should still be limited to small portions of whole grains—to about one cup maximum per meal. Even though some grains can have high protein content, the focus should still be on leafy vegetables. Beans are another good inclusion, but starchy beans should be avoided. However, lentils and other similar beans are good for you as they are great for introducing fiber, protein, and minerals into one's diet. But these should be cooked thoroughly to limit the kind of digestion problems that one may end up having thanks to bean consumption.

Avoid processed sugars

While sugar need not be totally eliminated from one's diet, processed sugars should be avoided as much as possible, as the Pegan Diet aims to steer us away from anything that could spike insulin production and elevate blood sugar. However, this does not mean one is banned from eating sugary things. Still, consumption should be extremely limited, and this should be seen as a treat and not a regular item in your diet.

Limit dairy consumption

What people who adhere to the Vegan Diet or the Paleo Diet end up missing the most is dairy. Dairy products are some of the favorite food items of people worldwide. The fact that paleo and vegan diets limit this is one hump that many people have a hard time getting over. In the case of the Pegan Diet, dairy is permissible. However, thanks to the high impact dairy has on the environment due to its production process, it is advised that it be consumed in limited amounts and, as much as possible, sourced from sustainable sources. However, dairy is a good protein source and can be treated as such.

Avoid chemicals and preservatives

As much as possible, chemicals and preservatives should be avoided in foods. This includes chemical additives, preservatives, dyes, artificial sweeteners, or other junk ingredients. GMO foods are all right, though natural foods are better. However, as GMO foods are meant to make production more efficient, with more food produced relative to the land used, they also improve sustainability. However, GMO foods also tend to go through a lot of processing, so they should still be consumed in limited amounts.

Choose sustainably produced foods

As much as possible, food should be grown sustainably. However, this is more for the health of the planet and the environment than for personal health. As much as possible, organic, grass-fed, and pasture-raised meats should be used. When it comes to fish, wild fish is always preferable due to the less dangerous chemicals, such as mercury, in them. Again, one must ensure that their food is sourced sustainably.

The Combined Health Benefits of the Pegan Diet

There are many benefits of a Pegan diet, with weight loss being the number one positive outcome. But there are other benefits too, and when these things work together, not only does that help drop the number on the scale, but it aids in clearer thinking and helps lead to an overall healthier, happier life. This is no exaggeration. The Pegan Diet seamlessly combines the best components of both diets and creates something really special.

Takes weight off effortlessly

That last word is no joke. Science reports that sugar and carbohydrates are stored as fat if they're not used immediately. On the flip side, healthy fats—a pillar of the Pegan Diet—do not get stored as fat because they are not processed in your liver. In fact, the body prefers to use fat as an energy source over carbohydrates or simple sugars, at least for the long haul. So, unless you're running marathons or working out for hours each day, you're never going to burn off those stored calories from sugar and unhealthy carbs. On top of that, many people merely sit at a desk all day.

However, eating the Pegan way is not just about calories in/calories out. It's more about what kind of calories and when. It's focusing on the quality of our food choices versus the number of our food choices. You heard it right: no calorie counting! And it really works. In the early days of putting this book together, when I took my own advice a little more closely, I lost the last few pounds I had wanted to get rid of for a while. And they have stayed off, too.

Helps to reduce belly fat

Here's the other kicker: eating too many processed foods and not enough whole, fresh foods, as we now know, can lead to chronic inflammation in the body. Chronic inflammation is at the foundation of developing potentially harmful diseases and causes cortisol levels to spike, putting you in a state of constant stress. The unfortunate reaction to that hormone imbalance is stored visceral fat. This bad fat collects around major organs and expands waistlines. By focusing on a colorful variety of fresh, whole foods in their purest form, while minimizing dairy, you can prevent these hormonal shifts from producing belly fat. And—you guessed it—by shedding belly fat, you also shed the pounds.

While exercise is not the focus of this book, adding even a minimal amount of strength training to your routine will boost the power of a Pegan lifestyle. You will notice more muscle definition. Compared to belly fat, lean muscle mass burns calories more efficiently throughout the day. This is imperative; not just for weight loss but for weight maintenance once you reach your goal.

Helps you with food cravings

Have you ever experienced out-of-control cravings for Ben & Jerry's ice cream, pizza at any time of the day, bagels, bready sandwiches, or chocolate, chocolate, and more chocolate in any form? Admittedly, those were my crazy cravings before I shifted into a paleo, then Pegan, lifestyle. There's a reason why these high-protein, low-carb, low- or no-sugar diets work. Carbohydrates and any form of sugar, even in the form of an artificial sweetener, cause insulin levels to spike. Suppose you eat carbs or sugars frequently throughout the day. In that case, even if it's in the form of what is considered to be healthy—orange juice, whole-wheat toast, or gluten-free pasta—your insulin level remains high throughout the day and even into the night. In incidences of prediabetes and type 2 diabetes, this can lead to insulin resistance.

For the record, vegetables are carbs, too. However, they don't have the same impact on blood sugar because of their high fiber count. That said, beans and grains are also high in fiber; they have many hard-to-burn starchy carbs, too, which is why the Pegan Diet outlines optimal choices and encourages moderation in this category. Carb consumption has addiction-like characteristics; it leads to cravings for more and more carbs (so don't blame your lack of willpower). Like alcohol abuse, too much insulin can lead to a fatty liver. Double yikes.

Helps to regulate your appetite

Too much insulin also causes problems with appetite control by blocking leptin in the brain. You'll think you're hungry, even if your body has all the energy it needs. By not stressing over calories and simply focusing on choosing high-quality fresh, whole foods the majority of the time, you'll see how much your body will naturally regulate your appetite every time you sit down to a meal or eat on the run. You will remember what it really feels like to be truly hungry and be able to give your body only what it needs. You will also become more familiar with what it feels like to actually be full. However, the Pegan Diet is about eating until you're just about full, not stuffed. And it's kind of hard to stuff yourself on broccoli, right? When your ability to perceive a sense of fullness improves, you will likely eat less in general, which, you guessed it, leads to more weight loss!

Makes you less lethargic and clears up mental fog

The energy boost you'll feel when you kick processed carbs and sugars to the curb is life-changing. At least, it was for me. Two things cause this: The lack of sugar in your diet helps ward off those erratic, emotional, addiction-like behaviors and cravings for unhealthy foods; also, by increasing our intake of foods rich in omega-3 fatty acids, such as avocados, walnuts, grass-fed beef and butter, and low-mercury fish, we're actually sending energy to and feeding our brain. Neurons crave fat; when you fuel them with it, they fire better. Recent studies show that healthy fats are not just great for heart health; they are actually more important for brain and nerve health. Besides the mental clarity you will experience, eating vegetables and other foods in their natural state will provide you with more energy to fuel your day than you ever imagined.

Improves your gut health

You might be hearing more about probiotics and gut flora, and there's a reason for that. Scientists, dietitians, doctors, and nutritionists see the connection between poor gut health and everything from digestive tract problems to disease development, weight gain, and belly fat. These experts report that most people have low amounts of good bacteria and high amounts of bad bacteria in their intestines. That's not our fault, though. It has more to do with the way food is grown in the United States and how drugs are prescribed or, perhaps, overprescribed. Soil health, especially in nonorganic plots, is not great in this country, to the extent that even organic farms have had to work hard to develop the proper levels of nitrogen to grow fruits and vegetables with nutritional adequacy.

There are toxins in many forms in the environment, from pollutants in the air you breathe to the water—including carbon-filtered water—you drink, and even from the furniture you sit on. You need more pre-and probiotics, or the good bacteria, to fight off these toxins and stay regular in your gut flora. Sure, there are probiotics in fortified dairy products such as yogurt and kefir. Still, these products tend to have a lot of sugar, not to mention nonpastured dairy sources. You can obtain just as many good probiotics from a wider variety of fruits and vegetables and antioxidant-rich prebiotics such as onions, leeks, garlic, and others in the Alum family. I also like to take a refrigerated probiotic pill each morning on an empty stomach to ensure I'm getting all I need.

Helps with good cholesterol

Your total cholesterol level may rise after eating the Pegan way for some time, as was the case for me. That's likely due to the rise in healthy cholesterol levels (HDLs), even if the bad cholesterol levels (LDLs) stay the same or, better yet, go down. As we now know, neither saturated fat nor eggs are the villains they once were portrayed.

Processed foods and oils, sugar, and processed carbs have been linked to high blood pressure and unhealthy cholesterol levels, which can cause heart disease. So, go ahead and eat that healthy fat—just make sure to choose pastured proteins and nontoxic fish to ensure you're getting omega-3 fatty acids, not the inflammatory omega-6 fatty acids found in meat from corn-fed animals and in processed foods.

Improves your palate

Try cutting out sugar completely for a week, and you'll notice how sickeningly sweet anything with sugar becomes, even certain fruits! This is also true of salt. When you scale back on restaurant food and cook your own meals using good-quality salt in moderation, you will soon notice how overly salty things can taste when dining out. The good news is that contemporary chefs are starting to veer away from salty toward savory and acidic flavors. After adopting the Pegan diet, even once-detested broccoli has become a favorite for me. There are so many ways to develop the flavor of food without extra salt or sweeteners. This can be achieved by adding a little extra garlic and onion, which are powerful cancer-fighting antioxidants. Also healthful are fresh or dried herbs, spices for heat, fat in the form of healthy oils and butter, and acid in the form of roasted tomatoes, vinegar, or a splash of citrus. Nuts and seeds round out a dish with that nice crunchy texture we crave— no need to look for that in chips anymore. When these foods are combined, they hit all your senses, proving that healthy is also very delicious.

Re-invigorates your skin

This is a fun one. When I cut out sugar and unhealthy carbs, save for treats on rare occasions, I noticed that I didn't have to wear as much foundation and that my skin actually glowed and softened a little. The Pegan Diet improves your skin by increasing quality fats, foods rich in Vitamin E (such as avocados), collagen in Homemade Bone Broth, pastured bone-in meats (yes, it's OK to gnaw on a bone as our paleo ancestors did!), and beta carotene found in orange- and deep-colored vegetables.

Helps to change your lifestyle

Eating the Pegan way will dramatically change your life for the better. As you can see, you will not only look and feel better, but you will also become better equipped to tackle life's many challenges, both mental and physical. That sounds like a tall order but making wise food choices and refocusing your goals will free you up from all the time spent wondering what, when, and how to eat, while fueling your body and brain with the ingredients they need to perform at their best level. No more yo-yo dieting and fleeting results. Your new Best You will become the Permanent You.

Chapter 4: The Pegan Diet Starter Guide

Now that you have a pretty clear idea of what the Pegan Diet comprises, this chapter will briefly explain the steps involved when starting to follow this path for the first time.

The provided 2-week meal plan in this chapter is designed to allow you to integrate all of this diet's benefits in a short period. The meal plan will encourage you to follow a more organized food routine, by eliminating harmful foods that might increase your blood sugar and replacing them with healthier alternatives.

Once you are done with the 2-week session, though, you will have the option to continue down this path, or you may decide to re-incorporate the foods that are being cut from your diet, one at a time.

You Should Plan for Success

Before you begin, you should know that following the Pegan lifestyle requires a bit more cooking and prepping than most of the other diets because you are essentially preparing your mind to adopt a completely new way of thinking and cooking.

If possible, you may even consider doing some batch cooking, which means that you choose one or two days a week and prepare the ingredients/meals for the next few days on one seating. Afterward, you will be able to enjoy your healthy meal without any hassle.

This might take some time getting used to, but you will eventually be able to get good at it, and it will become second nature to you.

I have a dedicated chapter where I give you an elementary breakdown of how to approach meal planning. But right now, let me walk you through what ingredients you should have in your pantry before starting the 2-week journey.

Setting Up Your Pegan Pantry

The first step toward embracing the Pegan lifestyle is to stock up your kitchen pantry and fridge according to your diet requirements. Keep in mind that the following is by no means an exhaustive list, but it should give you an idea of the most essential items you will need.

Choose wisely from them, based on the types of meals you will prepare, instead of just running out and buying everything at once.

I tried to keep the list as simple as possible, so you should be able to get most, if not all, of the items at your local grocery store.

Core Products

- Red apples
- Artichoke hearts, water-packed
- Avocados
- Baby spinach, fresh
- Basil, fresh
- Beets
- Bell peppers—green, yellow, or orange
- Berries of different colors, such as strawberries, raspberries, blueberries
- Bok choy
- Cabbage—red or Napa
- Carrots
- Celery

- Chard, Swiss
- Chives, fresh
- Cilantro, fresh
- Collard greens
- Cucumber
- Eggplant
- Garlic
- Ginger
- Green beans
- Kale
- Lemons
- Lettuce—Boston, red leaf, or romaine
- Limes
- Mushrooms
- Olives
- Onions—yellow or red
- Oregano, fresh
- Parsley, flat-leaf
- Peppers—jalapeno or serrano
- Rosemary, fresh
- Squash—butternut, spaghetti, acorn, yellow, or summer
- Scallions
- Shallots
- Sweet potatoes
- Tomatoes, fresh
- Tomatillos
- Zucchini

Meat and Poultry

- Beef, grass-fed
- Bison, grass-fed

- Butter, grass-fed
- Chicken—pastured or organic
- Eggs—pastured or organic
- Game—elk or venison
- Lamb, pastured and grass-fed
- Pork, pastured or crate-free
- Turkey, pastured

Seafood

- Arctic char, wild
- Cod
- Clams, canned or fresh
- Crab, canned or fresh
- Flounder
- Herring, wild-caught
- Lobster
- Mackerel, Atlantic or Pacific
- Mussels
- Oysters
- Salmon—wild-caught, fresh or canned
- Sardines, fresh or canned
- Scallops
- Shrimp
- Snapper
- Tilapia
- Trout
- Tuna, line-caught and fresh

Nuts and Seeds

- Almond butter, raw/dry roasted, unsalted
- Almonds, raw
- Brazil nuts, raw

- Cashew butter, roasted and unsalted
- Cashews, raw
- Chia seeds
- Flaxseeds
- Hazelnuts, raw or dry-roasted, unsalted
- Macadamia nuts—raw or dry-roasted, unsalted
- Pecans, raw and unsalted
- Pine nuts, from Italian sources
- Pistachios—raw or dry-roasted, unsalted
- Pumpkin seeds—raw or dry-roasted, unsalted
- Sesame seeds, toasted
- Walnut oil
- Walnuts—whole, chopped or raw/unsalted

Pantry Essentials

- Avocado oil
- Broth or stock, unsalted
- Cacao powder, raw
- Coconut flakes, unsweetened
- Coconut oil
- Dates, Medjool
- Honey, raw
- Hot sauce, no additives
- Maple syrup, no additives
- Miso
- Mustard, Dijon
- Nori sheets
- Nutritional yeast
- Olive oil, extra virgin, cold-pressed
- Salsa, no sugar or additives
- Sesame oil

- Soy sauce—gluten-free, Tamari, or coconut aminos
- Sriracha
- Tempeh
- Tofu, sprouted
- Tomatoes, no sugar or salt added
- Vanilla, extra pure/no alcohol
- Vinegars—balsamic/red wine/cider /sherry/coconut/rice
- Wasabi paste

Spices and Herbs

- Bay leaves
- Black pepper
- Cayenne pepper
- Chili powder
- Cinnamon, ground
- Cumin, ground
- Curry powder
- Garlic powder
- Nutmeg, whole
- Onion powder
- Oregano, dried
- Paprika, hot
- Red pepper flakes
- Salt
- Thyme, dried
- Turmeric

Setting Up Your Pegan Kitchen

Suppose this is your first time attempting to follow a diet. In that case, there are certain elements that you might need in your kitchen, as they would significantly help you in your journey. Keep in mind that this is by no means an exhaustive list, but if you can manage to gather this equipment, then preparing the ingredients and recipes you need will be a total breeze.

Cutting Boards: Try to get boards made from solid materials such as plastic, glass, rubber, or marble! These are mostly corrosion-resistant, and the non-porous surface makes these easier to clean than wooden boards.

Tools and equipment: The most basic ones include:

Measuring cups: Required to measure out spices and condiments

Various-sized spoons: Allow you to measure out small amounts of spices

Glass bowls: Required for storing meat as it's being marinated

Non-metallic containers: These can be used to store meat in the fridge

Kitchen and paper towels: Good for messes and draining meat

Cold storage space: The fridge will suffice since meats must be kept under 40 degrees Fahrenheit

Knives: Sharp knives should be used for meat slicing. While using the knife, you should keep the following in mind...

- Always make sure to use a sharp knife.

- Never hold a knife under your arm or leave it under a piece of meat.
- Always keep your knives within visible distance.
- Always keep your knifepoint down.
- Always cut down toward the cutting surface and away from your body.
- Never allow children to play with knives.
- Wash the knives between cutting different types of food.

Mesh gloves for protection: Cutting meat requires precision as you will be using a very sharp knife. The following types of gloves should be kept in mind:

- Rubber gloves
- Butchering gloves
- Mesh glove

Kitchen Scale for measurement: Allows you to get accurate measurements of condiments and small pieces of meat

Baking Sheet: Rectangular metal pan used in the oven, mainly for baking flat items such as sheet cakes, cookies, etc.

Colander: A bowl-shaped kitchen utensil with holes, which allows you to drain foods such as pasta or rice. These are also used to rinse veggies.

Aluminum Foil: Also known (incorrectly) as tin foil, this is used to wrap up and cover food

A Note on Choosing Your Containers

Storage containers lie at the heart of any diet as they allow you to store your food for later on. So, it's important that you understand the different types of containers available for purchase, as specific containers are suitable for certain tasks.

Choosing the proper container in your meal planning is crucial. In the long run, it will significantly determine the quality and flavor of the food you are storing.

That being said, this section should help you to avoid, at least a little bit, any problems by choosing the best container for your meals ahead of time.

Perhaps two of the most common materials used for containers are plastic and glass. (stainless steel is also considered later in this section). So, let's start by outlining the core difference between these two types of materials when looking at them from a meal prepper's point of view!

Facts about glass containers

- Glass containers are a bit more expensive but are ideal for long-term storage.
- Due to their heavy weight, glass containers are not ideal for "on-the-go" eating.
- They are generally easier to clean.
- If you are concerned about plastic safety, then these are the ones to go with!

Facts about plastic containers

- They're easy to carry and lightweight, ideal for individuals who are always on the go.

- They are more convenient and come in a wide variety of sizes and shapes.
- They are easy to dispose of.

Those are the individual differences between glass and plastic containers; the following points are general notes that you should keep in mind while choosing any container.

- When considering containers for freezing, a good practice is to go with containers designed to sustain extreme temperatures. Even though freezing is a really good option for long-term storage, an improper container will expose your food to "freezer burn" (white patches on food that destroy flavor). Thick-glassed mason jars are good options along with freezer-safe zip bags.

- Stainless steel containers are excellent for preventing freezer burn and are great for storing smoothie-type foods or meals with meat.

- Make sure to buy containers that are leakproof and have a tight lid. Some containers come with "snap-on" lids, which is a pretty good option. But if you are on a tight budget, you can also go for some common containers from good brands such as Rubbermaid or Glad.

- Always make sure to buy containers that are clearly labeled "microwave safe." Aside from the fact that normal containers might instantly melt in your microwave, they might also hamper the texture and flavor of your meal and make it unappealing in the long run. However, if you want to avoid the risk of plastic flavor altogether, go for glass containers!

The 14-Day Meal Plan

Keep in mind that the following meal plan is designed to act as a template that you can either follow or use to create your own arrangement by substituting the wide variety of recipes found in this book.

I tried to keep the meal plan as simple as possible so that you can effortlessly pull it off. In that light, I offer three different meals for breakfast, lunch, dinner, and snacks for each week and repeated them over the course of the week.

This will allow you easily plan the week using the awesome instructions provided in this book, and it ensures that you don't have to go through too much of a hassle. Once you have mastered meal planning, you may opt for more advanced meal plans, with a different type of meal every single day if you wish.

Regardless of how you decide to approach it, the main idea to always keep in mind is that you should try to go for as many fruits and vegetables as possible, keeping your meat consumption at a moderate level.

Day	Breakfast	Lunch	Dinner	Snacks
1	1.Overnight Chia Pudding	37.Almond Breaded Chicken	27.Perfect Cucumber Gazpacho	94.Cool Avocado Chips
2	3.Lovely Avocado Baked-Eggs	42.Blackened Chicken	25.Awesome Garlic and Kale	95.Exotic Cucumber Sushi
3	18.Roasted Garlic Soup	82.Walnut Encrusted Salmon	30.Lovely Tomato Salad	93Lemon Broccoli Roast
4	1.Overnight Chia Pudding	37.Almond Breaded Chicken	27.Perfect Cucumber Gazpacho	94.Cool Avocado Chips

5	3.Lovely Avocado Baked-Eggs	42.Blackened Chicken	25.Awesome Garlic and Kale	95.Exotic Cucumber Sushi
6	18.Roasted Garlic Soup	82.Walnut Encrusted Salmon	30.Lovely Tomato Salad	93.Lemon Broccoli Roast
7	1.Overnight Chia Pudding	37.Almond Breaded Chicken	27.Perfect Cucumber Gazpacho	94.Cool Avocado Chips
8	12.Chia and Flax Porridge	20.Cauliflower and Mushroom Risotto	86.Baked Halibut	99.Walnuts and Asparagus Combo
9	15.Coconut and Hazelnut Chiller	21.Brussels Lemon Delight	69.Caramelized Pork Chops	97.Onion and Thyme Crackers
10	8.Peanut Butter and Cocoa Smoothie	32.Creamy Mushroom Soup	60.Cabbage Fried Beef	92.Cool and Warm Beans Dish
11	12.Chia and Flax Porridge	20.Cauliflower and Mushroom Risotto	86.Baked Halibut	99.Walnuts and Asparagus Combo
12	15.Coconut and Hazelnut Chiller	21.Brussels Lemon Delight	69.Caramelized Pork Chops	97.Onion and Thyme Crackers
13	8.Peanut Butter and Cocoa Smoothie	32.Creamy Mushroom Soup	60.Cabbage Fried Beef	92.Cool and Warm Beans Dish
14	15.Coconut and Hazelnut Chiller	21.Brussels Lemon Delight	69.Caramelized Pork Chops	97.Onion and Thyme Crackers

What to Expect After 14 Days

Once you are done with the 2-week meal plan, you might find yourself in a situation where you are asking yourself what you can expect now.

Well, the Pegan Diet's whole idea is basically to re-orient the craving system of your body so that you desire more and more healthy foods as opposed to processed and unhealthy ones. So, after two weeks there remains a possibility that you might end up desiring more and more salad, fruits, and vegetables.

This happens because after those two weeks your body has already re-aligned itself to the new feeding pattern and is sending signals to your brain, letting you know what nutrients and vitamins you need.

When it comes to the Pegan Diet, you are in control of what you eat. If you can follow the Pegan for 90-95% of the time, when you suddenly get a craving for pizza you don't need to feel bad about it. Consume the pizza and enjoy every last bite of it without feeling any guilt! But afterward, try to continue following the Pegan way until your next craving hits you.

Pegan is a very flexible and efficient way of leading your life—one that does not require too much effort but bears extraordinarily healthy benefits if followed properly.

A Note on Dining Out, Pegan Style

The Pegan lifestyle doesn't mean that you don't get to dine out anymore! However, there are certain pointers that you should keep in mind:

- When dining out and you choose a salad, make sure to request a dressing of just olive oil and a squeeze of lemon.
- Try to skip meat at the most fast-food joints unless they have clearly stated that their proteins are grass-fed and organic.
- Try to avoid sauteed vegetables and ask for steamed to avoid processed oil.
- Watch out for dishes that are labeled "creamy," "breaded," or "crusted," as these were likely made using flour or breadcrumbs.
- Know that most commercially made soups use flour, cornstarch, or other forms of thickeners and a high amount of salt, both of which are unhealthy.
- If opting for a burger, try to ask for extra lettuce and eat your burger without the bun.
- Try to avoid the breadbasket.

Chapter 5: The Meal Planning Guide

What Exactly is Meal Prep?

In the most common terms, meal prepping's core objective is to give you a blueprint, or an outline if you will, that will guide you as to how you can make meal preparations for your diet.

That being said, the most general definition of the term is: "Meal prepping is the process of planning what you are going to eat (and how you are going to make it) ahead of time."

The Advantages of Meal Prep

But before we move along any further, you must be very curious as to why you should put so much effort into preparing meals, right? Let me break down some of the core benefits below for your convenience.

- Meal prepping helps you to control your portions by adjusting a set amount of food per meal; this gives you greater control over what you eat, helping in weight loss as well.
- Greater control of your food routine will help you create a more balanced and nutritious diet plan in the long run.
- Since everything is pre-planned, it will help you to avoid the rush of "last-minute preparations" and make the cooking process easier for you.
- Meal prepping will help you seamlessly multitask between other important tasks instead of staying in the kitchen all day to cook. Since you will keep everything prepared, it will save a lot of time in your daily routine and allow you to focus on other activities.

- Prepping prevents wasting time by letting you know exactly "What" you will eat and "When."
- It helps you avoid monotony in your daily meals by spicing up the routine from time to time.
- It helps you to save money by allowing you to set up a rough estimate of your food budget ahead of time.
- It allows you to stick to a healthy plan and eat as much healthy food as possible.
- It minimizes food wastage.

And a lot more.

The Very Basics of Meal Prep

You should understand that there is a very close relationship between meal prepping and meal planning. This is exactly why most people often mix these up and get confused. Let me clear this up for you.

Meal planning is essentially the process of creating an outline of what you will eat over some time. On the other hand, meal prepping is how you will prepare the ingredients for the meals you are going to make.

Keeping that in mind, at its core there are four basic steps to creating your very own meal plan.

Step 1: Choose a Day

The first step for creating a meal prep guide is to choose the day when you will prepare the ingredients. Weekends are perfect since you will be able to get the most out of your day. Plus, if you are a family person, then your family members can help you as well.

More experienced meal preppers tend to go for Sunday and Wednesday as their preparing days and divide the total work between these two days.

When beginning, though, you should not plan meals for the whole week, as it might be too much to do! Try to prepare three meals at the beginning and keep increasing the number as you become more proficient.

Step 2: Choose Your Meals

The next step is to choose the meals you will prepare for breakfast, lunch, and dinner. If you are preparing for the whole family, dinner meals will be where most of your efforts will go.

When choosing the recipes, you should try to maintain your specific macronutrient goal, depending on your guide (protein, fats, and carbs are to be considered).

Once you have decided on your meals, the next step is to make a shopping list of the ingredients you will need.

Step 3: Equipment and Shopping List

As an example, let's assume that we have the following ingredients:

- 2 large bags of mixed vegetables such as broccoli, carrots, cauliflower, etc.
- 2 and ½ pounds of sweet potatoes

- Salt and pepper as needed, along with any seasoning mix that you might want

As for the equipment:

- 2 baking sheets
- Aluminum foil, as needed
- Large cooking pot
- Colander
- Cutting board
- Knife
- Non-stick cooking spray
- Containers such as plastic containers or bags

Remember, all of the equipment has already been discussed in the previous chapter.

Step 4: The Process

Keep in mind that the meal prepping process will vary from one meal to the next; the instructions below are simply for following the ingredient list provided above.

- Take a large pot, add your vegetables and water, and boil the vegetables properly (covered)
- Wash the potatoes thoroughly, peel, and cut them into nice rounds
- Take a baking tray and cover the bottom with a baking sheet; transfer potato rounds to the baking dish and bake for 30 minutes
- The veggies should be boiled by now, so strain them using a colander
- Take different containers and add the veggies to the containers; portion them out as needed

- Once the sweet potatoes are done, do the same with the potatoes
- Season the veggies with salt and pepper and cover.

And that's about it!

The template above gives you an idea of how meal plans are made; you can use this template to create your own meal plan based on your diet and requirements.

Leave a 1-Click Review!

If you find this book usefull I would be incredibly thankful if you could take just 60 seconds to write a brief review on Amazon, even if it's just a few sentences!

>> Scan with your camera to leave a quick review:

Thank you and I can't wait to see your thoughts.

Chapter 6: Breakfast and Brunch Recipes[1]

1. Awesome Overnight Chia Pudding (Vegan)

Preparation Time: 5 minutes/Cooking Time: No Cook Time/Serves: 1 Serving

Nutrition Per Serving: Carbohydrates: 21 grams/Fat: 19 grams/Protein: 10 grams/Fiber: 3 grams/Calories: 293

---

[1] A quick note before we start with recipes. To keep our books at a reasonable price for you, we print in black & white. That was mentioned in book description that you are buying black & white version. Hovewer, you can get a PDF copy of colourfull recipe pictures from this link: http://bit.ly/101pictures (totaly free and no registration required!)

Ingredients

- 3 tablespoons of chia seeds
- 1 cup of coconut milk
- 1 teaspoon alcohol-free vanilla extract
- 1 teaspoon maple syrup

Directions

1. Take a large bowl and add all of the listed ingredients; gently stir and close the lid
2. Transfer to your fridge and let it refrigerate overnight
3. Next morning, serve with your desired toppings

2. Healthy Pancakes With Berry Syrup (Vegetarian)

Preparation Time: 2 minutes/Cooking Time: 10 minutes/Serves: 3 Servings (3 Pancakes Per Serving)

Nutrition Per Serving: Carbohydrates: 18 grams/Fat: 17 grams/Protein: 4 grams/Fiber: 3 grams/Calories: 224

Ingredients

- 1 large banana, ripe
- 2 large whole eggs
- 1 tablespoon alcohol-free vanilla extract
- 1 teaspoon ground cinnamon
- Pinch of salt
- ¼ cup clarified butter/coconut oil
- 2 cups fresh blueberries
- Additional cherries/strawberries for topping (optional)

Directions

1. Take a medium-sized bowl, add the banana and mash it until tender
2. Add eggs and keep mashing until you have a smooth batter
3. Stir in vanilla, cinnamon, and salt
4. Take a large skillet and place it over medium heat; add 1 tablespoon of coconut oil and let it heat up
5. Add 2-3 tablespoons batter to form about 3-inch rounds
6. Cook 4 pancakes at a time, making sure to cook them for about 3-4 minutes; flip them once until both sides are browned
7. Keep repeating until all of the batter has been used up, making sure to add 1 tablespoon of oil to the skillet between batches
8. Take another small saucepan and add blueberries along with the remaining 1 tablespoon of coconut oil
9. Cook over medium heat, making sure to continually mash the berries with a wooden spoon until the juices are reduced to a syrup-like consistency. It should take about 3-5 minutes
10. Put the mix aside and let it cool
11. Serve your pancakes with the blueberry syrup on the side and some cut cherries/ strawberries on top
12. Enjoy!

Storage Tips: You may freeze the extra pancakes, but separate them with parchment paper before storing them. You may keep them for 2 months in the fridge.

3. Lovely Avocado Baked-Eggs (Vegetarian | Low-Carb)

Preparation Time: 5 minutes/Cooking Time: 15 minutes/Serves: 2 servings

Nutrition Per Serving: Carbohydrates: 16 grams/Fat: 37 grams/Protein: 16 grams/Fiber: 4 grams/Calories: 433

Ingredients

- 2 medium or large avocados, halved or pitted
- 4 large whole eggs
- ¼ teaspoons fresh ground black pepper

Directions

1. Preheat your oven to 425 degrees F
2. Scoop out some pulp from the avocado halves, leaving enough space to fit an egg
3. Line an 8 x 8-inch baking pan with foil, place avocado halves in the pan to fit nicely in a single layer

4. Gently fold the foil around the outer edges of the avocados
5. Crack 1 egg into each avocado half, season them with pepper
6. Bake for about 12-15 minutes uncovered until you have your desired doneness
7. Remove from oven and let them rest for 5 minutes
8. Serve and enjoy!

4. Healthy Nut Porridge (Vegan)

Preparation Time: 5 minutes/Cooking Time: 15 minutes/Serves: 2 Servings

Nutrition Per Serving: Carbohydrates: 12 grams/Fat: 22 grams/Protein: 6 grams/Fiber: 2 grams/Calories: 260

Ingredients

- 1 cup cashew nuts, raw and unsalted
- 1 cup pecans, halved
- 2 tablespoons stevia
- 4 teaspoons coconut oil, melted
- 2 cups of water

Directions

1. Chop the nuts in a food processor to form a smooth paste
2. Add water, oil, and stevia to nut paste and transfer the mix to a saucepan
3. Stir and cook for 5 minutes on high heat
4. Lower heat and simmer for 10 minutes
5. Serve warm and enjoy!

5. Flaxseed Porridge (Vegan|Low-Carb)

Preparation Time: 15 minutes/Cooking Time: Nil/Serves: 2 Servings

Nutrition Per Serving: Carbohydrates: 5 grams/Fat: 13 grams/Protein: 16 grams/Fiber: 2 grams/Calories: 259

Ingredients

- 2 tablespoons coconut flour
- 2 tablespoons vanilla protein powder
- 3 tablespoons golden flaxseed meal
- 1 and ½ cups almond milk, unsweetened
- Powdered erythritol

Directions

1. Take a bowl and mix in the flaxseed meal, protein powder, and coconut flour; mix well
2. Add mix to the saucepan (placed over medium heat)
3. Add almond milk and stir, letting the mixture thicken
4. Add your desired amount of sweetener and serve; add some berries as a topping
5. Enjoy!

6. Cool Green Smoothie (Vegan)

Preparation Time: 10 minutes/Cooking Time: Nil/Serves: 2 Servings

Nutrition Per Serving: Carbohydrates: 18 grams/Fat: 23 grams/Protein: 10 grams/Fiber: 2 grams/Calories: 309

Ingredients

- 1 cup plant milk
- 1 pack stevia
- 1 tablespoon coconut flakes, unsweetened
- 1 cup of water
- 2 cups spring mix salad
- 1 tablespoon coconut oil

Directions

1. Add listed ingredients to a blender
2. Blend until you have a smooth and creamy texture
3. Serve chilled and enjoy!

7. Chilled Cinnamon Smoothie (Vegan|Low-Carb)

Preparation Time: 10 minutes/Cooking Time: Nil/Serves: 2 Servings

Nutrition Per Serving: Carbohydrates: 1.6 grams/Fat: 4 grams/Protein: 0.6 grams/Fiber: 0.2 grams/Calories: 145

Ingredients

- 1 cup unsweetened almond milk
- 2 tablespoons vanilla protein powder
- ½ teaspoon cinnamon
- ¼ teaspoon vanilla extract
- 1 tablespoon chia seeds
- 1 cup ice cubes

Directions

1. Add listed ingredients to a blender
2. Blend until you have a smooth and creamy texture
3. Serve chilled and enjoy!

8. Peanut Butter and Cocoa Smoothie (Vegan|Low-Carb)

Preparation Time: 5 minutes/Cooking Time: Nil/Serves: 2 Servings

Nutrition Per Serving: Carbohydrates: 6 grams/Fat: 24 grams/Protein: 33 grams/Fiber: 2 grams/Calories: 604

Ingredients

- 1 cup water
- 1/3 cup heavy whip cream
- 1/3 cup chocolate whey protein, low carb
- 2 ice cubes
- 2 tablespoons peanut butter

Directions

1. Add the listed ingredients to your blender and blend until you have a smooth mixture
2. Chill and enjoy!

9. Excellent No-Bake Breakfast Cookies (Vegan|Low-Carb)

Preparation Time: 5 minutes/Cooking Time: 5 minutes/Serves: 2 Servings

Nutrition Per Serving: Carbohydrates: 4.6 grams/Fat: 14 grams/Protein: 5 grams/Fiber: 2 grams/Calories: 159

Ingredients

- ¼ cup coconut oil
- ¼ cup cocoa powder
- 1/3 cup stevia
- ½ cup peanut butter
- ½ cup coconut, shredded
- 1 cup almonds, flaked

Directions

1. Take a baking tray and line it with greased baking paper
2. Take a bowl and add the flaked almonds and coconut; mix well
3. Take a small saucepan and add peanut butter, cocoa, stevia, and coconut oil
4. Place the pan over medium heat and gently stir until the mixture is creamy and smooth
5. Pour chocolate peanut mix over almonds
6. Stir well until you have a nice cookie dough
7. Spread out the dough over a baking tray, transfer to your fridge
8. Let the cookies harden for a while
9. Serve and enjoy!

10. Morning Strawberry Chia Jam (Vegan|Low-Carb)

Preparation Time: 5 minutes/Cooking Time: 5 minutes/Serves: 2 Servings

Nutrition Per Serving: Carbohydrates: 4 grams/Fat: 20 grams/Protein: 9 grams/Fiber: 4 grams/Calories: 214

Ingredients

- ¼ cup stevia
- ¼ cup chia seeds
- 1 and ¼ pounds strawberries, frozen

Directions

1. Transfer the frozen berries into a small saucepan and place it over medium-high heat
2. Gently keep on stirring the berries until they are soft; mash them carefully
3. Once they are smooth, add chia and stevia to the mix and gently stir
4. Adjust the flavor and serve
5. Enjoy!

11. Healthy Raspberry Smoothie (Vegan)

Preparation Time: 2 minutes/Cooking Time: 2 minutes/Serves: 2 Servings

Nutrition Per Serving: Carbohydrates: 10 grams/Fat: 1.3 grams/Protein: 6 grams/Fiber: 2 grams/Calories: 83

Ingredients

- ½ cup coconut milk + ¾ cup almond milk
- ¼ cup raspberries
- ¼ cup coconut yogurt

Directions

1. Take a bowl and mix in flaxseed meal, protein powder, and coconut flour; mix well
2. Add mix to the saucepan (placed over medium heat)
3. Add almond milk and stir, letting the mixture thicken
4. Add your desired amount of sweetener and serve
5. Enjoy!

12. Chia and Flax Porridge (Vegan)

Preparation Time: 5 minutes/Cooking Time: 5-10 minutes/Serves: 2 Servings

Nutrition Per Serving: Carbohydrates: 10 grams/Fat: 38 grams/Protein: 6 grams/Fiber: 2 grams/Calories: 410

Ingredients

- 1 tablespoon chia seeds
- 1 tablespoon ground flaxseed
- 1/3 cup coconut cream
- ½ cup water
- 1 teaspoon vanilla extract
- 1 tablespoon butter

Directions

1. Add chia seeds, coconut cream, flaxseed, water, and vanilla to a small pot
2. Stir and let it sit for 5 minutes
3. Add butter and place pot over low heat
4. Keep stirring as butter melts
5. Once the porridge is hot (not boiling), pour it into a bowl
6. Enjoy!
7. Add a few berries or a dash of cream for extra flavor

13. Vanilla Hemp Drink (Vegan)

Preparation Time: 5 minutes/Cooking Time: Nil/Serves: 2 Servings

Nutrition Per Serving: Carbohydrates: 10 grams/Fat: 20 grams/Protein: 7 grams/Fiber: 3 grams/Calories: 250

Ingredients

- 1 cup unsweetened hemp milk, vanilla
- 1 and ½ tablespoons coconut oil, unrefined
- ½ cup frozen blueberries, mixed
- 4 cups leafy greens, kale, and spinach
- 1 tablespoon flaxseeds
- 1 tablespoon almond butter

Directions

1. Add listed ingredients to a blender
2. Blend until you have a smooth and creamy texture
3. Garnish with some shredded coconut, if desired
4. Serve chilled and enjoy!

14. Macadamia Protein Smoothie (Vegan|Low-Carb)

Preparation Time: 5 minutes/Cooking Time: Nil /Serves: 2 Servings

Nutrition Per Serving: Carbohydrates: 1 gram/Fat: 2 grams/Protein: 12 grams/Fiber: 0 grams/Calories: 165

Ingredients

- 2 tablespoons macadamia nuts, salted
- 1/3 cup chocolate whey protein powder, low carb
- 1 cup almond milk, unsweetened

Directions

1. Add the listed ingredients to your blender and blend until you have a smooth mixture
2. Chill and enjoy!

15. Coconut and Hazelnut Chiller (Vegan)

Preparation Time: 5 minutes/Cooking Time: 15 minutes/Serves: 2 Servings

Nutrition Per Serving: Carbohydrates: 12 grams/Fat: 46 grams/Protein: 7 grams/Fiber: 4 grams/Calories: 457

Ingredients

- ½ cup coconut milk
- ¼ cup hazelnuts, chopped
- 1 and ½ cups water
- 1 pack stevia

Directions

1. Add listed ingredients to a blender
2. Blend until you have a smooth and creamy texture
3. Serve chilled and enjoy!

16. Flavorful Breakfast Hash (Vegan)

Preparation Time: 5 minutes/Cooking Time: 15 minutes/Serves: 2 Servings

Nutrition Per Serving: Carbohydrates: 5 grams/Fat: 10 grams/Protein: 3 grams/Fiber: 1 gram/Calories: 126

Ingredients

- 1 tablespoon parsley
- ¼ cup red bell pepper, diced
- ½ teaspoon black pepper
- ½ teaspoon salt
- ½ teaspoon garlic powder
- ½ teaspoon paprika
- 1 tablespoon olive oil
- 1 cup Brussel sprouts, halved
- ¼ onion, diced
- 1 large turnip, peeled and diced

Directions

1. Take a large skillet and place it over medium-high heat
2. Add turnips and season with spices, cook for about 5-7 minutes making sure to stir from time to time
3. Add onion and Brussel sprouts; cook for 3 minutes more until tender
4. Add red bell pepper and cook for 5 minutes more
5. Garnish with a bit of parsley and serve
6. Enjoy!

17. Awesome Strawberry Shake (Vegetarian)

Preparation Time: 10 minutes/Cooking Time: Nil/Serves: 2 Servings

Nutrition Per Serving: Carbohydrates: 15 grams/Fat: 46 grams/Protein: 4 grams/Fiber: 2 grams/Calories: 470

Ingredients

- ½ cup heavy cream, liquid
- 1 tablespoon cocoa powder
- 1 pack stevia
- ½ cup strawberry, sliced
- 1 tablespoon coconut flakes, unsweetened
- 1 and ½ cups water

Directions
1. Add listed ingredients to a blender
2. Blend until you have a smooth and creamy texture
3. Serve chilled and enjoy!

18. Cinnamon and Coconut Porridge (Vegetarian|Low-Carb)

Preparation Time: 5 minutes/Cooking Time: 5 minutes/Serves: 2 Servings

Nutrition Per Serving: Carbohydrates: 6 grams/Fat: 16 grams/Protein: 2 grams/Fiber: 4 grams/Calories: 171

Ingredients

- 2 cups water
- 1 cup 36% heavy cream
- ½ cup unsweetened dried coconut, shredded
- 2 tablespoons flaxseed meal
- 1 tablespoon butter
- 1 and ½ teaspoons stevia
- 1 teaspoon cinnamon
- Salt to taste
- Blueberries for topping

Directions

1. Add the listed ingredients to a small pot, mix well
2. Transfer the pot to the stove and place it over medium-low heat
3. Bring the mix to a slow boil
4. Stir well and remove from heat
5. Divide the mix into equal servings and let them sit for 10 minutes
6. Top with your desired toppings and enjoy!

Chapter 7: Plant-Based Mains

19. Green Beans and Onion Roast (Vegan|Low-Carb)

Preparation Time: 5 minutes/Cooking Time: 15 minutes/Serves: 3 Servings

Nutrition Per Serving: Carbohydrates: 4 grams/Fat: 20 grams/Protein: 9 grams/Fiber: 2 grams/Calories: 214

Ingredients

- 1 yellow onion, sliced into rings
- ½ teaspoon onion powder
- 2 tablespoons coconut flour
- 1 and 1/3 pounds fresh green beans, trimmed and chopped
- ½ tablespoon salt

Directions

1. Take a large bowl and mix salt with onion powder and coconut flour
2. Add onion rings
3. Mix well to coat
4. Spread the rings on a baking sheet lined with parchment paper
5. Drizzle with some oil
6. Bake for 10 minutes at 400 Fahrenheit
7. Parboil the green beans for 3 to 5 minutes in the boiling water
8. Drain and serve the beans with baked onion rings
9. Serve warm and enjoy!

20. Cauliflower and Mushroom Risotto (Vegan)

Preparation Time: 5 minutes/Cooking Time: 15 minutes/Serves: 4 Servings

Nutrition Per Serving: Carbohydrates: 15 grams/Fat: 17 grams/Protein: 12 grams/Fiber: 4 grams/Calories: 438

Ingredients

- 4 and ½ cups cauliflower, riced
- 3 tablespoons coconut oil
- 1 pound Portobello mushrooms, thinly sliced
- 1 pound white mushrooms, thinly sliced
- 2 shallots, diced
- ¼ cup organic vegetable broth
- Salt and pepper to taste
- 3 tablespoons chives, chopped
- 4 tablespoons butter
- ½ cup parmesan cheese, grated

Directions

1. Use a food processor and pulse cauliflower florets until riced
2. Take a large saucepan and heat up 2 tablespoons oil over medium-high flame
3. Add mushrooms and sauté for 3 minutes until mushrooms are tender
4. Clear saucepan of mushrooms and liquid and keep them on the side
5. Add the remaining 1 tablespoon of oil to the skillet
6. Toss shallots and cook for 60 seconds
7. Add cauliflower rice and stir for 2 minutes until coated with oil
8. Add broth to riced cauliflower and stir for 5 minutes
9. Remove pot from heat and mix in mushrooms and liquid
10. Add chives, butter, and parmesan cheese
11. Season with salt and pepper
12. Serve and enjoy!

21. Brussels Lemon Delight (Vegan| Low-Carb)

Preparation Time: 10 minutes/Cooking Time: Nil/Serves: 3 Servings

Nutrition Per Serving: Carbohydrates: 9 grams/Fat: 36 grams/Protein: 7 grams/Fiber: 3 grams/Calories: 382

Ingredients

- 1 pound Brussels sprouts, trimmed and shredded
- 8 tablespoons olive oil
- 1 lemon, juiced and zested
- Salt and pepper to taste
- ¾ cup spicy almond and seed mix

Directions

1. Take a bowl and mix in lemon juice, salt, pepper, and olive oil
2. Mix well
3. Stir in shredded Brussels and toss
4. Let it sit for 10 minutes
5. Add nuts and toss
6. Serve and enjoy!

22. Skillet Kale and Avocado (Vegetarian|Low-Carb)

Preparation Time: 5 minutes/Cooking Time: 10 minutes/Serves: 4 Servings

Nutrition Per Serving: Carbohydrates: 6 grams/Fat: 34 grams/Protein: 18 grams/Fiber: 4 grams/Calories: 461

Ingredients

- 2 tablespoons olive oil, divided
- 2 cups mushrooms, sliced
- 5 ounces fresh kale, stemmed and sliced into ribbons
- 1 avocado, sliced
- 4 large whole eggs
- Salt and pepper as needed

Directions

1. Take a large skillet and place it over medium heat
2. Add a tablespoon of olive oil
3. Add mushrooms to the pan and sauté for 3 minutes
4. Take a medium bowl and massage kale with the remaining 1 tablespoon olive oil for about 1-2 minutes
5. Add kale to skillet and place it on top of mushrooms
6. Place slices of avocado on top of the kale
7. Create 4 wells for eggs and crack each egg onto each hole
8. Season eggs with salt and pepper
9. Cover skillet and cook for 5 minutes
10. Serve hot!

23. Almond and Blistered Beans (Vegan|Low-Carb)

Preparation Time: 5 minutes/Cooking Time: 15 minutes/Serves: 2 Servings

Nutrition Per Serving: Carbohydrates: 6 grams/Fat: 16 grams/Protein: 45 grams/Fiber: 3 grams/Calories: 347

Ingredients

- 1 pound fresh green beans, ends trimmed
- 1 and ½ tablespoons olive oil
- ¼ teaspoon salt
- 1 and ½ tablespoons fresh dill, minced
- Juice of 1 lemon
- ¼ cup crushed almonds
- Salt as needed

Directions

1. Preheat your oven to 400 degrees F
2. Add in the green beans with your olive oil and also the salt
3. Spread them in one single layer on a large sheet pan
4. Roast it for 10 minutes; stir it nicely and roast for another 8-10 minutes
5. Remove it from the oven and keep stirring in the lemon juice along with the dill
6. Top with crushed almonds and some flaky sea salt and serve

Chapter 8: Vegetarian Soups, Salads, and Snacks

24. Coconut and Cauliflower Rice Delight (Vegan|Low-Carb)

Preparation Time: 5 minutes/Cooking Time: 20 minutes/Serves: 3 Servings

Nutrition Per Serving: Carbohydrates: 4 grams/Fat: 7 grams/Protein: 1 gram/Fiber: 2 grams/Calories: 95

Ingredients

- 3 cups cauliflower, riced
- 2/3 cup full-fat coconut milk
- 1 to 2 teaspoons sriracha paste
- ¼ to ½ teaspoon onion powder
- Salt as needed
- Fresh basil for garnish

Directions

1. Take a pan and place it over medium-low heat
2. Add all of the ingredients and stir them until fully combined
3. Cook for about 5-10 minutes, making sure that the lid is on
4. Remove the lid and keep cooking until any excess liquid goes away
5. Once the rice is soft and creamy, enjoy!

25. Awesome Garlic and Kale (Vegan|Low-Carb)

Preparation Time: 5 minutes/Cooking Time: 10 minutes/Serves: 2 Servings

Nutrition Per Serving: Carbohydrates: 5 grams/Fat: 8 grams/Protein: 4 grams/Fiber: 2 grams/Calories: 121

Ingredients

- 1 bunch kale
- 2 tablespoons olive oil
- 4 garlic cloves, minced

Directions

1. Carefully tear the kale into bite-sized portions, making sure to remove the stems
2. Discard the stems
3. Take a large pot and place it over medium heat
4. Add olive oil and let the oil heat up
5. Add garlic and stir for 2 minutes
6. Add kale and cook for 5-10 minutes
7. Serve!

26. BBQ'd Zucchini Delight (Vegan|Low-Carb)

Preparation Time: 10 minutes/Cooking Time: 60 minutes/Serves: 3 Servings

Nutrition Per Serving: Carbohydrates: 4 grams/Fat: 7 grams/Protein: 1 gram/Fiber: 1 gram/Calories: 95

Ingredients

- Olive oil, as needed
- 3 zucchinis
- ½ teaspoon black pepper
- ½ teaspoon mustard
- ½ teaspoon cumin
- 1 teaspoon paprika
- 1 teaspoon garlic powder
- 1 tablespoon of sea salt
- 1 to 2 stevia packets
- 1 tablespoon chili powder

Directions

1. Preheat your oven to 300 degrees F
2. Take a small bowl and add cayenne, black pepper, salt, garlic, mustard, paprika, chili powder, and stevia
3. Mix well
4. Slice zucchini into 1/8-inch slices and mist them with olive oil
5. Sprinkle spice blend over zucchini and bake for 40 minutes
6. Remove and flip, mist with more olive oil and leftover spice
7. Bake for 20 minutes more
8. Serve!

27. Perfect Cucumber-Tomato Gazpacho (Vegan)

Preparation Time: 5-7 minutes/Cooking Time: No Cook Time /Serves: 2 Servings

Nutrition Per Serving: Carbohydrates: 20 grams/Fat: 34 grams/Protein: 4 grams/Fiber: 3 grams/Calories: 376

Ingredients

- 8 ripe plum/heirloom tomatoes
- 1 medium red bell pepper, seeded and coarsely chopped
- 1 medium cucumber, coarsely chopped
- ½ cup extra virgin olive oil
- 1 tablespoon balsamic/red wine vinegar
- Salt and pepper, as needed
- Sunflower seeds for garnish

Directions

1. Take your food processor and add tomatoes, pepper, cucumber; pulse until everything breaks down
2. While the motor is still running, add oil and continue to process for about 2 minutes until the mix is smooth and velvety
3. Add vinegar and process for a few seconds more
4. Refrigerate the soup for about 2 hours; serve cold with a bit of salt and pepper
5. Garnish with some seeds if desired
6. Enjoy!

Storage Tips: You may keep this soup for 5 days in the fridge and 3 months in the freezer.

28. Cool Healthy Guacamole (Vegan)

Preparation Time: 15 minutes/Cooking Time: Nil/Serves: 3 Servings

Nutrition Per Serving: Carbohydrates: 11 grams/Fat: 15 grams/Protein: 16 grams/Fiber: 2 grams/Calories: 172

Ingredients

- 3 large ripe avocados
- 1 large red onion, peeled and diced
- 4 tablespoons of freshly squeezed lime juice
- Salt as needed
- Freshly ground black pepper as needed
- Cayenne pepper as needed

Directions

1. Halve the avocados and discard the stones
2. Scoop flesh from the avocado halves and transfer to a large bowl
3. Mash using a fork
4. Add 2 tablespoons of lime juice and mix
5. Dice the remaining avocado flesh (remaining half) and transfer to another bowl
6. Add remaining juice and toss
7. Add diced flesh with the mashed flesh and mix
8. Add chopped onions and toss
9. Season with salt, pepper, and cayenne pepper
10. Serve and enjoy!

29. Hearty Tomato Platter (Vegetarian)

Preparation Time: 10 minutes/Cooking Time: Nil/Serves: 3 Servings

Nutrition Per Serving: Carbohydrates: 8 grams/Fat: 22 grams/Protein: 2 grams/Fiber: 3 grams/Calories: 233

Ingredients

- 1/3 cup olive oil
- 1 teaspoon salt
- 2 tablespoons onion, chopped
- ¼ teaspoon pepper
- ½ a garlic, minced
- 1 tablespoon fresh parsley, minced
- 3 large fresh tomatoes, sliced
- 1 teaspoon dried basil
- ¼ cup red wine vinegar

Directions
1. Take a shallow dish and arrange tomatoes in the dish
2. Add the rest of the ingredients to a mason jar, cover the jar, and shake it well
3. Pour mix over tomato slices
4. Let it chill for 2-3 hours
5. Serve!

30. Lovely Tomato Salad (Low-Carb|Vegan)

Preparation Time: 5 minutes/Cooking Time: 25 minutes/Serves: 3 Servings

Nutrition Per Serving: Carbohydrates: 4.5 grams/Fat: 10 grams/Protein: 12 grams/Fiber: 2 grams/Calories: 115

Ingredients

- ½ cup scallions, chopped
- 1 pound cherry tomatoes
- 3 teaspoons olive oil
- Sea salt and freshly ground black pepper, to taste
- 1 tablespoon red wine vinegar

Directions

1. Season tomatoes with spices and oil
2. Heat your oven to 450 degrees Fahrenheit
3. Take a baking sheet and spread the tomatoes
4. Bake for 15 minutes
5. Stir and turn the tomatoes
6. Bake for another 10 minutes
7. Take a bowl and mix the roasted tomatoes with all the remaining ingredients
8. Serve and enjoy!

31. Perfect Veggie Packed Soup (Low-Carb|Vegan)

Preparation Time: 10 minutes/Cooking Time: Nil/Serves: 2 Servings

Nutrition Per Serving: Carbohydrates: 6 grams/Fat: 7 grams/Protein: 3 grams/Fiber: 2 grams/Calories: 100

Ingredients

- 1 avocado, pitted and chopped
- 1 cucumber, chopped
- 2 bunches spinach
- 1 and ½ cups watermelon, chopped
- 1 bunch cilantro, roughly chopped
- Juice from 2 lemons
- ½ cup coconut aminos
- ½ cup lime juice

Directions

1. Add cucumber and avocado to your blender and pulse well
2. Add cilantro, spinach, and watermelon; blend
3. Add lemon, lime juice, and coconut amino
4. Pulse a few more times
5. Transfer to a soup bowl and enjoy!

32. Creamy Mushroom Soup (Vegan|Low-Carb)

Preparation Time: 5 minutes/Cooking Time: 30 minutes/Serves: 2 Servings

Nutrition Per Serving: Carbohydrates: 5 grams/Fat: 17 grams/Protein: 4 grams/Fiber: 2 grams/Calories: 200

Ingredients

- 1 tablespoon olive oil
- ½ large onion, diced
- 20 ounces mushrooms, sliced
- 6 garlic cloves, minced
- 2 cups vegetable broth
- 1 cup coconut cream
- ¾ teaspoon salt
- ¼ teaspoon black pepper

Directions

1. Take a large pot and place it over medium heat
2. Add onion and mushrooms in olive oil and sauté for 10-15 minutes
3. Make sure to keep stirring it from time to time until it's browned evenly
4. Add garlic and sauté for 10 minutes more
5. Add vegetable broth, coconut cream, coconut milk, black pepper, and salt
6. Bring it to a boil and bring down the temperature to low
7. Simmer for 15 minutes
8. Use an immersion blender to puree the mixture
9. Enjoy!

33. Awesome Kale and Spinach Bowl (Vegan|Low-Carb)

Preparation Time: 5 minutes/Cooking Time: 10 minutes/Serves: 2 Servings

Nutrition Per Serving: Carbohydrates: 7 grams/Fat: 13 grams/Protein: 5 grams/Fiber: 2 grams/Calories: 124

Ingredients

- 3 ounces of coconut oil
- 8 ounces kale, chopped
- 2 avocados, diced
- 4 and 1/3 cups of coconut milk
- Salt and pepper to taste

Directions

1. Take a skillet and place it over medium heat
2. Add kale and sauté for 2-3 minutes
3. Add kale to the blender
4. Add water, spices, coconut milk, and avocado to the blender as well
5. Blend until smooth and pour the mix into a bowl
6. Serve and enjoy!

34. Roasted Garlic Soup (Vegan|Low-Carb)

Preparation Time: 5 minutes/Cooking Time: 60 minutes/Serves: 4 Servings

Nutrition Per Serving: Carbohydrates: 4 grams/Fat: 8 grams/Protein: 4 grams/Fiber: 2 grams/Calories: 142

Ingredients

- 1 tablespoon olive oil
- 2 bulbs garlic, peeled
- 3 shallots, chopped
- 1 large head of cauliflower, chopped
- 6 cups vegetable broth
- Salt and pepper to taste

Directions

1. Preheat your oven to 400 degrees F
2. Slice ¼-inch off the top of the garlic bulb and place this in aluminum foil
3. Grease with olive oil and roast in the oven for 35 minutes
4. Squeeze flesh out of the roasted garlic
5. Heat oil in a saucepan and add shallots; sauté for 6 minutes
6. Add garlic and remaining ingredients
7. Cover the pan and bring down the heat to low
8. Let it cook for 15-20 minutes
9. Use an immersion blender to puree the mixture
10. Season soup with salt and pepper
11. Serve and enjoy!

35. The Perfect Zucchini Bowl (Low-Carb|Vegan)

Preparation Time: 5 minutes/Cooking Time: 20 minutes/Serves: 3 Servings

Nutrition Per Serving: Carbohydrates: 4 grams/Fat: 2 grams/Protein: 7 grams/Fiber: 2 grams/Calories: 160

Ingredients

- 1 onion, chopped
- 3 zucchinis, cut into medium chunks
- 2 tablespoons coconut milk
- 2 garlic cloves, minced
- 4 cups vegetable stock
- 2 tablespoons coconut oil
- Pinch of salt
- Black pepper to taste

Directions

1. Take a pot and place it over medium heat
2. Add oil and let it heat up
3. Add zucchini, garlic, and onion; stir
4. Cook for 5 minutes
5. Add stock, salt, and pepper; stir
6. Bring to a boil and then lower the heat
7. Simmer for 20 minutes. Remove from the heat and add coconut milk
8. Use an immersion blender until smooth
9. Ladle into soup bowls and serve
10. Enjoy!

36. Asparagus and Walnuts Sauté (Low-Carb|Vegan)

Preparation Time: 5 minutes/Cooking Time: 5 minutes/Serves: 3 Servings

Nutrition Per Serving: Carbohydrates: 2 grams/Fat: 12 grams/Protein: 3 grams/Fiber: 2 grams/Calories: 124

Ingredients

- 1 and ½ tablespoons olive oil
- ¾ pound asparagus, trimmed
- ¼ cup walnuts, chopped
- Salt and pepper to taste

Directions

1. Place a skillet over medium heat, add olive oil and let it heat up
2. Add asparagus, sauté for 5 minutes until browned
3. Season with salt and pepper
4. Remove from heat
5. Add walnuts and toss
6. Serve warm!

Chapter 9: Chicken and Poultry

37. Almond Breaded Chicken (Low-Carb)

Preparation Time: 5 minutes/Cooking Time: 15 minutes/Serves: 2 Servings

Nutrition Per Serving: Carbohydrates: 3 grams/Fat: 24 grams/Protein: 16 grams/Fiber: 2 grams/Calories: 325

Ingredients

- 2 large chicken breasts, boneless and skinless
- 1/3 cup lemon juice
- 1 and ½ cups seasoned almond meal
- 2 tablespoons coconut oil
- Lemon pepper, to taste
- Parsley for decoration

Directions

1. Slice chicken breasts in half
2. Pound out each half until ¼ inch thick
3. Take a pan and place it over medium heat, add oil, and heat it up
4. Dip each chicken breast slice into lemon juice and let it sit for 2 minutes
5. Turn over and let the other side sit for 2 minutes as well
6. Transfer to almond meal and coat both sides
7. Add coated chicken to the oil and fry for 4 minutes per side, making sure to sprinkle lemon pepper on liberally
8. Transfer to a paper-lined sheet and repeat until all chicken is fried
9. Garnish with parsley and enjoy!

38. Blackberry Chicken Wings (Low-Carb)

Preparation Time: 30 minutes/Cooking Time: 50 minutes/Serves: 5 Servings

Nutrition Per Serving: Carbohydrates: 1.8 grams/Fat: 39 grams/Protein: 34 grams/Fiber: 1 gram/Calories: 502

Ingredients

- 3 pounds chicken wings, about 20 pieces
- ½ cup blackberry chipotle jam
- Salt and pepper to taste
- ½ cup water

Directions

1. Add water and jam to a bowl and mix well
2. Place chicken wings in a plastic bag and add two-thirds of the marinade
3. Season with salt and pepper
4. Let it marinate for 30 minutes
5. Preheat your oven to 400 degrees F
6. Prepare a baking sheet and wire rack, place chicken wings in the wire rack, and bake for 15 minutes
7. Brush remaining marinade and bake for 30 minutes more
8. Enjoy!

39. Lettuce Turkey Wrap (Low-Carb)

Preparation Time: 5 minutes/Cooking Time: 10 minutes/Serves: 4 Servings

Nutrition Per Serving: Carbohydrates: 7 grams/Fat: 4 grams/Protein: 23 grams/Fiber: 2 grams/Calories: 162

Ingredients

- 1 and ¼ pounds of ground turkey, lean
- 4 green onions, minced
- 1 tablespoon of olive oil
- 1 garlic clove, minced
- 2 teaspoons of chili paste
- 8-ounce water chestnut, diced
- 3 tablespoons of hoisin sauce
- 2 tablespoons of coconut aminos

- 1 tablespoon of rice vinegar
- 12 butter lettuce leaves
- 1/8 teaspoon of salt

Directions

1. Take a pan and place it over medium heat; add turkey and garlic to the pan
2. Heat for 6 minutes until cooked
3. Take a bowl and transfer turkey to the bowl
4. Add onions and water chestnuts
5. Stir in hoisin sauce, coconut aminos, vinegar, and chili paste
6. Toss well and transfer the mix to lettuce leaves
7. Serve and enjoy!

40. Chicken Dinner Casserole (Low-Carb)

Preparation Time: 5 minutes/Cooking Time: 50 minutes/Serves: 4Servings

Nutrition Per Serving: Carbohydrates: 9 grams/Fat: 23 grams/Protein: 33 grams/Fiber: 2 grams/Calories: 378

Ingredients

- 4 chicken breast halves, skinless and boneless
- 1 pound okra
- 1 big onion, chopped
- 2 cups diced, undrained canned tomatoes
- 5 garlic cloves, crushed
- 1 teaspoon paprika
- Salt and pepper, as needed

Directions

1. Preheat your oven to 350 degrees F
2. Take a large baking dish and place it over medium heat
3. Add oil and let the oil heat up
4. Add onion and sauté for 2 minutes
5. Add paprika, pepper, garlic; sauté for 2 minutes more
6. Stir in okra and tomatoes; remove from heat and arrange chicken pieces into the veggies
7. Season with salt and pepper
8. Cover and bake for 40 minutes
9. Gently stir about halfway through
10. Serve and enjoy!

41. Chicken and Basil With Zucchini Zoodles

Preparation Time: 5 minutes/Cooking Time: 10 minutes/Serves: 2 Servings

Nutrition Per Serving: Carbohydrates: 13 grams/Fat: 27 grams/Protein: 59 grams/Fiber: 2 grams/Calories: 540

Ingredients

- 2 chicken fillets, cubed
- 2 tablespoons ghee
- 1 pound tomatoes, diced
- ½ cup basil, chopped
- ¼ cup coconut milk
- 1 garlic clove, peeled and minced
- 1 zucchini, shredded

Directions

1. Sauté cubed chicken in ghee until no longer pink
2. Add tomatoes and season with salt
3. Simmer and reduce the liquid
4. Prepare your zucchini noodles by shredding zucchini in a food processor
5. Add basil, garlic, coconut milk to chicken and cook for a few minutes
6. Add half of the zucchini zoodles to a bowl and top with creamy tomato basil chicken
7. Enjoy!

42. Blackened Chicken (Low-Carb)

Preparation Time: 5 minutes/Cooking Time: 10 minutes/Serves: 2 Servings

Nutrition Per Serving: Carbohydrates: 1 gram/Fat: 3 grams/Protein: 24 grams/Fiber: 2 grams/Calories: 136

Ingredients

- ½ teaspoon paprika
- 1/8 teaspoon salt
- ¼ teaspoon cayenne pepper
- ¼ teaspoon ground cumin
- ¼ teaspoon dried thyme
- 1/8 teaspoon ground white pepper
- 1/8 teaspoon onion powder
- 2 chicken breasts, boneless and skinless

Directions

1. Preheat your oven to 350 degrees Fahrenheit
2. Grease baking sheet
3. Take a cast-iron skillet and place it over high heat
4. Add oil and heat it up for 5 minutes until smoking hot
5. Take a small bowl and mix together salt, paprika, cumin, white pepper, cayenne, thyme, and onion powder
6. Oil the chicken breasts on both sides and coat them with the spice mix
7. Transfer to your hot pan and cook for 1 minute per side
8. Transfer to your prepared baking sheet and bake for 5 minutes
9. Serve and enjoy!

43. Stir-Fried Chicken Chow-Mein (Low-Carb)

Preparation Time: 5 minutes/Cooking Time: 15 minutes/Serves: 4 Servings

Nutrition Per Serving: Carbohydrates: 8 grams/Fat: 18 grams/Protein: 42 grams/Fiber: 4 grams/Calories: 368

Ingredients

- ½ cup onions, sliced
- 2 tablespoons sesame garlic-flavored oil
- 4 cups bok choy, shredded
- 3 stalks celery, chopped
- 1 and ½ teaspoons garlic, minced
- 1 cup chicken broth
- 2 tablespoons coconut aminos
- 1 tablespoon ginger, minced
- 1 teaspoon arrowroot
- 4 boneless chicken breasts, cooked and sliced

Directions

1. Add bok choy and celery in a skillet along with 1 tablespoon of garlic oil
2. Stir fry until the bok choy is tender
3. Add the rest of the ingredients except the arrowroot
4. If the mixture is too thin, pour a mixture of ½ a cup of cold water and arrowroot into the skillet
5. Bring the whole mixture to a 1-minute boil
6. Remove the heat source
7. Stir in coconut aminos and let it sit for 4 minutes until thick
8. Serve and enjoy!

44. Simple Parsley Chicken Breast (Low-Carb)

Preparation Time: 5 minutes/Cooking Time: 40 minutes/Serves: 4 Servings

Nutrition Per Serving: Carbohydrates: 4 grams/Fat: 4 grams/Protein: 25 grams/Fiber: 2 grams/Calories: 150

Ingredients

- 1 tablespoon dry parsley
- 1 tablespoon dry basil
- 4 chicken breast halves, boneless and skinless
- ½ teaspoon salt
- ½ teaspoon red pepper flakes, crushed
- 2 tomatoes, sliced

Directions

1. Preheat your oven to 350 degrees F
2. Take a 9 x 13-inch baking dish and grease it with cooking spray
3. Sprinkle 1 tablespoon of parsley and 1 teaspoon of basil over the mixture and spread the mixture into your baking dish
4. Arrange the chicken breast halves in the dish and sprinkle garlic slices on top
5. Take a small bowl and add 1 teaspoon parsley, 1 teaspoon basil, salt, and red pepper; mix well. Pour the mixture over the chicken breast
6. Top with tomato slices and cover; bake for 25 minutes
7. Remove the cover and bake for 15 minutes more
8. Serve and enjoy!

45. Spicy Chipotle Lettuce Chicken

Preparation Time: 5 minutes/Cooking Time: 25 minutes/Serves: 2 Servings

Nutrition Per Serving: Carbohydrates: 13 grams/Fat: 15 grams/Protein: 34 grams/Fiber: 4 grams/Calories: 332

Ingredients

- 1 pound chicken breast, cut into strips
- Splash of olive oil
- 1 red onion, finely sliced
- 14 ounces tomatoes
- 1 teaspoon chipotle, chopped
- ½ teaspoon cumin
- Pinch of sugar
- Lettuce, as needed

- Fresh coriander leaves
- Jalapeno chilies, sliced
- Fresh tomato slices for garnish
- Lime wedges

Directions

1. Take a non-stick frying pan and place it over medium heat
2. Add oil and heat it up
3. Add chicken and cook until brown
4. Keep the chicken on the side
5. Add tomatoes, sugar, chipotle, and cumin to the same pan and simmer for 25 minutes until you have a nice sauce
6. Add chicken to the sauce and cook for 5 minutes
7. Transfer the mix to another place
8. Use lettuce to wrap a portion of the mixture and serve with a squeeze of lemon
9. Enjoy!

46. Juicy Mustard Chicken

Preparation Time: 10 minutes/Cooking Time: 40 minutes/Serves: 4 Servings

Nutrition Per Serving: Carbohydrates: 10 grams/Fat: 23 grams/Protein: 64 grams/Fiber: 4 grams/Calories: 531

Ingredients

- 4 chicken breasts
- ½ cup chicken broth
- 3 to 4 tablespoons mustard
- 3 tablespoons olive oil
- 1 teaspoon paprika
- 1 teaspoon chili powder
- 1 teaspoon garlic powder

Directions

1. Take a small bowl and mix together the mustard, olive oil, paprika, chicken broth, garlic powder, chicken broth, and chili
2. Add chicken breasts and marinate for 30 minutes
3. Arrange the chicken on a lined baking sheet
4. Bake for 35 minutes at 375 degrees Fahrenheit
5. Serve and enjoy!

47. Buffalo Lettuce Wraps (Low-Carb)

Preparation Time: 10 minutes/Cooking Time: 35 minutes/Serves: 3 Servings

Nutrition Per Serving: Carbohydrates: 2 grams/Fat: 6 grams/Protein: 5 grams/Fiber: 4 grams/Calories: 106

Ingredients

- 3 chicken breasts, boneless and cubed
- 20 slices of butter lettuce leaves
- ¾ cup cherry tomatoes, halved
- 1 avocado, chopped
- ¼ cup green onions, diced
- ½ cup of ranch dressing
- ¾ cup hot sauce

Directions

1. Take a mixing bowl and add chicken cubes and hot sauce, mix
2. Place in the fridge and let it marinate for 30 minutes
3. Preheat your oven to 400 degrees Fahrenheit
4. Place coated chicken on a cookie pan and bake for 9 minutes
5. Assemble lettuce serving cups with equal amounts of lettuce, green onions, tomatoes, ranch dressing, and cubed chicken
6. Serve and enjoy!

48. Italian Herbed Balsamic Chicken (Low-Carb)

Preparation Time: 10 minutes/Cooking Time: 25 minutes/Serves: 6 Servings

Nutrition Per Serving: Carbohydrates: 7 grams/Fat: 7 grams/Protein: 23 grams/Fiber: 4 grams/Calories: 196

Ingredients

- 6 chicken breast halves, skinless and boneless
- 1 teaspoon garlic salt
- Ground black pepper
- 2 tablespoons olive oil
- 1 onion, thinly sliced
- 14 and ½ ounces tomatoes, diced
- ½ cup balsamic vinegar
- 1 teaspoon dried basil
- 1 teaspoon dried oregano
- 1 teaspoon dried rosemary
- ½ teaspoon dried thyme

Directions

1. Season both sides of your chicken breasts thoroughly with pepper and garlic salt
2. Take a skillet and place it over medium heat
3. Add some oil and cook your seasoned chicken for 3-4 minutes per side until the breasts are nicely browned
4. Add some onion and cook for another 3-4 minutes until the onions are browned
5. Pour the diced tomatoes and balsamic vinegar over your chicken and season with some rosemary, basil, oregano, and thyme
6. Simmer the chicken for about 15 minutes until they are no longer pink
7. Take an instant-read thermometer and check if the internal temperature gives a reading of 165 degrees Fahrenheit
8. If yes, then you are good to go!

49. Greek Chicken Breast (Low-Carb)

Preparation Time: 5 minutes/Cooking Time: 25 minutes/Serves: 4 Servings

Nutrition Per Serving: Carbohydrates: 2 grams/Fat: 57 grams/Protein: 27 grams/Fiber: 0.5 grams/Calories: 644

Ingredients

- 4 chicken breast halves, skinless and boneless
- 1 cup extra virgin olive oil
- 1 lemon, juiced
- 2 teaspoons garlic, crushed
- 1 and ½ teaspoons black pepper
- 1/3 teaspoon paprika

Directions

1. Cut 3 slits in the chicken breasts
2. Take a small bowl and whisk in olive oil, salt, lemon juice, garlic, paprika, and pepper; whisk for 30 seconds
3. Place chicken in a large bowl and pour marinade
4. Rub the marinade all over the meat, using your hand
5. Refrigerate overnight
6. Pre-heat grill to medium heat and oil the grate
7. Cook chicken in the grill until the center is no longer pink
8. Serve and enjoy!

50. Easy Stir-Fried Chicken

Preparation Time: 5 minutes/Cooking Time: 12 minutes/Serves: 2 Servings

Nutrition Per Serving: Carbohydrates: 10 grams/Fat: 2 grams/Protein: 32 grams/Fiber: 4 grams/Calories: 227

Ingredients

- 2 pieces (7 ounces each) chicken breast, skinless and boneless
- ¼ pound brown mushrooms
- 1 tablespoon virgin coconut oil
- ¼ onion, sliced thinly
- 1 large orange bell pepper
- 1 tablespoon soy sauce
- ¼ pound brown mushroom

Directions

1. Take a nonstick saucepan and add heat the coconut oil
2. Add soy sauce, mushrooms, chicken, and bell pepper
3. Stir fry for 8 to 10 minutes
4. Remove from the pan and serve
5. Enjoy!

51. Spinach Chicken Breast Salad (Low-Carb)

Preparation Time: 5 minutes/Cooking Time: 30 minutes/Serves: 4 Servings

Nutrition Per Serving: Carbohydrates: 3 grams/Fat: 11 grams/Protein: 6 grams/Fiber: 1 gram/Calories: 100

Ingredients

- 3 and ½ ounces of chicken breast
- 2 cups spinach
- 1 and ¾ ounces lettuce
- 1 bell pepper
- 2 tablespoons olive oil
- Lemon juice to taste

Directions

1. Boil chicken breast 12 to 15 minutes without adding salt; cut the meat into small strips
2. Put the spinach in boiling water for a few minutes, cut into small strips
3. Cut pepper into strips as well
4. Add everything to a bowl and mix with juice and oil
5. Serve!

Chapter 10: Beef Recipes

52. Asian Beef Steak (Low-Carb)

Preparation Time: 5 minutes/Cooking Time: 5 minutes/Serves: 4 Servings

Nutrition Per Serving: Carbohydrates: 4 grams/Fat: 23 grams/Protein: 28 grams/Fiber: 2 grams/Calories: 350

Ingredients

- 2 tablespoons sriracha sauce
- 1 tablespoon garlic, minced
- 1 tablespoon ginger, freshly grated
- 1 yellow bell pepper, cut into strips
- 1 red bell pepper, cut into thin strips
- 1 tablespoon sesame oil, garlic-flavored
- 1 tablespoon stevia

- ½ teaspoon curry powder
- ½ teaspoon rice wine vinegar
- 8 ounces of beef sirloin, cut into strips
- 2 cups baby spinach, stemmed
- ½ head of butter lettuce, torn

Directions

1. Add garlic, sriracha sauce, 1 teaspoon of sesame oil, rice wine vinegar, and stevia in a bowl
2. Mix well
3. Pour half of the mix into a zip bag and add steak; allow it to marinate
4. Assemble the brightly colored salad by layering the vegetables in two bowls in the following order: baby spinach, butter lettuce, two peppers on top
5. Remove the steak from the marinade and discard the liquid
6. Heat sesame oil in a skillet over medium heat and add steak; stir fry for 3 minutes
7. Transfer your cooked steak to the top of the salad
8. Drizzle the other half of your marinade mix
9. Sprinkle sriracha sauce on top and serve!

53. Avocado Beef Patties

Preparation Time: 5 minutes/Cooking Time: 15 minutes/Serves: 2 Servings

Nutrition Per Serving: Carbohydrates: 9 grams/Fat: 43 grams/Protein: 38 grams/Fiber: 4 grams/Calories: 568

Ingredients

- 1 pound of 85% lean ground beef
- 1 small avocado, pitted and peeled
- 2 slices of yellow cheddar cheese
- Salt, as needed
- Fresh ground black pepper, as needed

Directions

1. Pre-heat and prepare your broiler to be high
2. Divide beef into two equal-sized patties
3. Season the patties with salt and pepper according to taste
4. Broil the patties for 5 minutes per side
5. Transfer the patties to a platter and add cheese
6. Slice avocado into strips and place them on top of the patties
7. Serve and enjoy!

54. Fresh Thai Beef Dish (Low-Carb)

Preparation Time: 5 minutes/Cooking Time: 10 minutes/Serves: 2 Servings

Nutrition Per Serving: Carbohydrates: 3 grams/Fat: 15 grams/Protein: 19 grams/Fiber: 1 gram/Calories: 224

Ingredients

- 1 cup beef stock
- 4 tablespoons peanut butter
- ¼ teaspoon garlic powder
- ¼ teaspoon onion powder
- 1 tablespoon coconut aminos
- 1 and ½ teaspoons lemon pepper
- 1 pound beef steak, cut into strips
- Salt and pepper to taste
- 1 green bell pepper, seeded and chopped
- 3 green onions, chopped

Directions

1. Take a bowl and add peanut butter, stock, aminos, and lemon pepper; stir
2. Keep the mixture to one side
3. Take a pan and place it over medium-high heat
4. Add beef and season with salt, pepper, onion, garlic powder
5. Cook for 7 minutes
6. Add green pepper, stir cook for 3 minutes
7. Add peanut sauce and green onions
8. Stir cook for 1 minute
9. Divide between platters and serve
10. Enjoy!

55. Beef Zucchini Halves (Low-Carb)

Preparation Time: 5 minutes/Cooking Time: 35 minutes/Serves: 2 Servings

Nutrition Per Serving: Carbohydrates: 8 grams/Fat: 10 grams/Protein: 21 grams/Fiber: 3 grams/Calories: 222

Ingredients

- 2 garlic cloves, peeled and minced
- 1 teaspoon cumin
- 1 tablespoon coconut oil
- 1 pound ground beef
- ½ cup onion, chopped
- 1 teaspoon smoked paprika

- Salt and pepper to taste
- 3 zucchinis, sliced lengthwise, with the insides scooped out
- ¼ cup fresh cilantro, chopped
- ½ cup cheddar cheese, shredded
- 1 and ½ cups enchilada sauce
- Avocado, chopped
- Green onions, chopped
- Tomatoes, cored and chopped

Directions

1. Take a pan and place it over medium-high heat
2. Add oil and heat it up
3. Add onions and stir cook for 2 minutes
4. Add beef and stir for a few minutes
5. Add paprika, salt, pepper, cumin, and garlic; stir cook for 2 minutes
6. Transfer zucchini halves to a baking pan
7. Stuff each with the beef mix and pour the enchilada sauce on top
8. Sprinkle the cheddar on top
9. Bake (covered) for 20 minutes at 350 degrees F
10. Uncover and sprinkle with cilantro
11. Bake for 5 minutes more
12. Sprinkle avocado, green onions, and tomatoes on top
13. Serve and enjoy!

56. Beef and Tomato Squash (Low-Carb)

Preparation Time: 5 minutes/Cooking Time: 60 minutes/Serves: 4 Servings

Nutrition Per Serving: Carbohydrates: 4 grams/Fat: 7 grams/Protein: 10 grams/Fiber: 4 grams/Calories: 260

Ingredients

- 2 pounds acorn squash, pricked with a fork
- Salt and pepper to taste
- 3 garlic cloves, peeled and minced
- 1 onion, peeled and chopped
- 1 portobello mushroom, sliced
- 28 ounces canned tomatoes, diced
- 1 teaspoon dried oregano
- ¼ teaspoon cayenne pepper
- ½ teaspoon dried thyme
- 1 pound ground beef
- 1 green bell pepper, seeded and chopped

Directions

1. Preheat your oven to 400 degrees F
2. Take acorn squash and transfer to the lined baking sheet; bake for 40 minutes
3. Cut in half and let it cool
4. Deseed the squash
5. Take a pan and place it over medium-high heat; add meat, garlic, onion, and mushroom and stir cook until brown
6. Add salt, pepper, thyme, oregano, cayenne, tomatoes, and green pepper; stir
7. Cook for 10 minutes
8. Stuff squash halves with beef mix
9. Transfer to oven and bake for 10 minutes more
10. Serve and enjoy!

57. Juicy Beef Stuffed Bell Pepper (Low-Carb)

Preparation Time: 5 minutes/Cooking Time: 10 minutes/Serves: 2 Servings

Nutrition Per Serving: Carbohydrates: 4 grams/Fat: 23 grams/Protein: 28 grams/Fiber: 1 gram/Calories: 350

Ingredients

- 1 onion, chopped
- 2 tablespoons coconut oil
- 1 pound ground beef
- 1 red bell pepper, diced
- 2 cups spinach, chopped
- Salt and pepper to taste

Directions

1. Take a skillet and place it over medium heat
2. Add onion and cook until slightly browned
3. Add spinach and ground beef
4. Stir fry until done—the whole process should take about 10 minutes
5. Fill up the bell peppers with the mixture
6. Serve and enjoy!

58. Tamari Steak Salad (Low-Carb)

Preparation Time: 5 minutes/Cooking Time: 15 minutes/Serves: 3 Servings

Nutrition Per Serving: Carbohydrates: 4 grams/Fat: 37 grams/Protein: 33 grams/Fiber: 1 gram/Calories: 500

Ingredients

- 2 large bunches of salad greens
- 8-9 ounces beef steak
- ½ red bell pepper, sliced
- 6 to 8 cherry tomatoes, cut into halves
- 4 radishes, sliced
- 4 tablespoons olive oil
- ½ tablespoon fresh lemon juice
- 2 ounces gluten-free tamari sauce
- Salt as needed

Directions

1. Marinate steak in tamari sauce
2. Make the salad by adding bell pepper, tomatoes, radishes, salad green, oil, salt, and lemon juice to a bowl and tossing them well
3. Grill the steak to your desired doneness and transfer steak to the top of the salad platter
4. Let it sit for 1 minute and cut it crosswise
5. Serve and enjoy!

59. Zucchini and Beef Sauté (Low-Carb)

Preparation Time: 5 minutes/Cooking Time: 10 minutes/Serves: 4 Servings

Nutrition Per Serving: Carbohydrates: 5 grams/Fat: 40 grams/Protein: 31 grams/Fiber: 1 gram/Calories: 500

Ingredients

- 10 ounces beef, sliced into 1 to 2-inch strips
- 1 zucchini, cut into 2-inch strips
- ¼ cup parsley, chopped
- 3 garlic cloves, minced
- 2 tablespoons tamari sauce
- 4 tablespoons avocado oil

Directions

1. Add 2 tablespoons avocado oil in a frying pan over high heat
2. Place in strips of beef and brown for a few minutes on high heat
3. Once the meat is brown, add zucchini strips and sauté until tender
4. Once tender, add tamari sauce, garlic, and parsley; let them sit for a few minutes more
5. Serve immediately and enjoy!

60. Cabbage Fried Beef (Low-Carb)

Preparation Time: 5 minutes/Cooking Time: 15 minutes/Serves: 3 Servings

Nutrition Per Serving: Carbohydrates: 5 grams/Fat: 22 grams/Protein: 34 grams/Fiber: 2 grams/Calories: 360

Ingredients

- 1 pound beef, ground
- ½ pound bacon
- 1 onion
- 1 garlic clove, minced
- ½ head cabbage, sliced
- Salt and pepper to taste

Directions

1. Take a skillet and place it over medium heat
2. Add chopped bacon, beef, and onion until slightly browned
3. Transfer to a bowl and keep it covered
4. Add minced garlic and cabbage to the skillet and cook until slightly browned
5. Return the ground beef mixture to the skillet and simmer for 3-5 minutes over low heat
6. Serve and enjoy!

61. Mushroom and Mediterranean Steak

Preparation Time: 10 minutes/Cooking Time: 14 minutes/Serves: 3 Servings

Nutrition Per Serving: Carbohydrates: 11 grams/Fat: 30 grams/Protein: 21 grams/Fiber: 3 grams/Calories: 386

Ingredients

- 1 pound boneless beef sirloin steak, ¾ inch thick, cut into 4 pieces
- 1 large red onion, chopped
- 1 cup mushrooms
- 4 garlic cloves, thinly sliced
- 4 tablespoons olive oil
- ½ cup green olives, coarsely chopped
- 1 cup parsley leaves, finely cut

Directions

1. Take a large skillet and place it over medium-high heat
2. Add oil and let it heat up
3. Add beef and cook until both sides are browned, remove beef and drain fat
4. Add rest of the oil to skillet and heat it up
5. Add onions and garlic; cook for 2-3 minutes
6. Stir well
7. Add mushrooms and olives; cook until mushrooms are thoroughly done
8. Return beef to skillet and lower heat to medium
9. Cook for 3-4 minutes (covered)
10. Stir in parsley
11. Serve and enjoy!

62. Beef Pot Roast (Low-Carb)

Preparation Time: 5 minutes/Cooking Time: 7 hours/Serves: 4 Servings

Nutrition Per Serving: Carbohydrates: 0.9 grams/Fat: 9 grams/Protein: 24 grams/Fiber: 0.1 gram/Calories: 181

Ingredients

- 2 pounds beef pot roast, cut up
- 1 tablespoon olive oil
- 1 tablespoon thyme, dried
- ½ teaspoon oregano, dried
- 1 whole bay leaf
- 1 medium onion, sliced
- ½ teaspoon black pepper
- 1 teaspoon salt
- 3 cups of water

Directions

1. Take a bowl and add thyme, oregano, black pepper, and salt
2. Mix them well
3. Rub the mixture all over the cut-up pot roast
4. Place a skillet over heat
5. Put in the marinated pot roast and sear all sides
6. Put the remaining ingredients in the slow cooker
7. Add the seared pot roast
8. Cook for 7 hours
9. Serve and enjoy!

63. Stir-Fried Ground Beef (Low-Carb)

Preparation Time: 5 minutes/Cooking Time: 15 minutes/Serves: 3 Servings

Nutrition Per Serving: Carbohydrates: 6 grams/Fat: 17 grams/Protein: 32 grams/Fiber: 4 grams/Calories: 304

Ingredients

- 1 pound ground beef
- ½ medium onion, chopped
- 1 tablespoon coconut oil
- 1 tablespoon Chinese five spices
- 5 medium-sized mushrooms, sliced
- 2 kale leaves, chopped
- ½ cup broccoli, chopped
- ½ red bell pepper, chopped
- 1 tablespoon cayenne pepper, optional

Directions

1. Take a skillet, add coconut oil
2. Heat the oil over medium-high heat
3. Sauté the onion for one minute and add vegetables
4. Keep stirring constantly
5. Add the ground beef and the spices
6. Cook for 2 minutes and lower the heat
7. Cover the skillet and cook for 10 minutes
8. Now it's ready to serve
9. Enjoy!

64. Pepper Beef Steak Stir Fry (Low-Carb)

Preparation Time: 5 minutes/Cooking Time: 10 minutes/Serves: 4 Servings

Nutrition Per Serving: Carbohydrates: 4 grams/Fat: 20 grams/Protein: 26 grams/Fiber: 1 gram/Calories: 297

Ingredients

- 8 ounces sliced mushrooms
- 2 tablespoons tamari
- ½ cup beef broth
- ¼ cup onion, chopped
- 1 medium green bell pepper, cut into strips
- Salt and pepper to taste
- 1 garlic clove, minced
- 1 pound sirloin steak, cut into thin strips
- 1 tablespoon sesame oil

Directions

1. Take a large skillet and place it over medium-high heat
2. Add beef strips and garlic; cook until the beef is nicely browned
3. Season with salt and pepper
4. Remove the meat from the skillet and add pepper and onion; cook them until soft
5. Add broth, tamari, mushrooms
6. Cook and stir well until the mushrooms are tender
7. Stir in the beef and keep cooking until thoroughly done
8. Serve and enjoy once done!

65. Vegetable and Beef Steak With Chimichurri (Low-Carb)

Preparation Time: 5 minutes/Cooking Time: 15 minutes/Serves: 6 Servings

Nutrition Per Serving: Carbohydrates: 9 grams/Fat: 34 grams/Protein: 25 grams/Fiber: 2 grams/Calories: 443

Ingredients

- ½ cup Chimichurri sauce
- 2 tablespoons olive oil
- 1 medium red onion, peeled and cut into eighths
- 1 medium yellow bell pepper, seeded and cut into large chunks
- 1 medium red bell pepper, seeded and cut into large chunks
- ¼ teaspoon ground black pepper
- 1 teaspoon salt
- 1 pound beef tri-tip steak, cut into 1-inch cubes

Directions

1. Season the steaks with salt and pepper
2. Thread steaks into skewers, alternating between the vegetables and meat. Brush with olive oil
3. Prepare your grill for high heat and grill your steak to the desired doneness, giving 2 to 3 minutes per side for a rare-medium doneness
4. Brush with more Chimichurri sauce and grill for 1 minute more
5. Serve and enjoy!

Chapter 11: Pork and Other Red Meats

66. Classical Mediterranean Pork (Low-Carb)

Preparation Time: 10 minutes/Cooking Time: 35 minutes/Serves: 4 Servings

Nutrition Per Serving: Carbohydrates: 2 grams/Fat: 2 grams/Protein: 26 grams/Fiber: 1 gram/Calories: 165

Ingredients

- 4 pork chops, bone-in
- Salt and pepper to taste
- 1 teaspoon dried rosemary
- 3 garlic cloves, peeled and minced

Directions

1. Season pork chops with salt and pepper
2. Place in roasting pan
3. Add rosemary and garlic to the pan
4. Preheat your oven to 425 degrees F
5. Bake for 10 minutes
6. Lower heat to 350 degrees F
7. Roast for 25 minutes more
8. Slice pork and divide on plates
9. Drizzle pan juice all over
10. Serve and enjoy

67. Bacon and Onion Pork Chops (Low-Carb)

Preparation Time: 10 minutes/Cooking Time: 45 minutes/Serves: 4 Servings

Nutrition Per Serving: Carbohydrates: 6 grams/Fat: 18 grams/Protein: 36 grams/Fiber: 2 grams/Calories: 325

Ingredients

- 2 onions, peeled and chopped
- 6 bacon slices, chopped
- ½ cup chicken stock
- Salt and pepper to taste
- 4 pork chops

Directions

1. Heat up a pan over medium heat and add bacon
2. Stir and cook until crispy
3. Transfer to bowl
4. Return pan to medium heat and add onions. Season with salt and pepper
5. Stir and cook for 15 minutes
6. Transfer to the bowl with the bacon
7. Return the pan to heat (medium-high) and add pork chops
8. Season with salt and pepper and brown for 3 minutes
9. Flip and lower heat to medium
10. Cook for 7 minutes more
11. Add stock and stir cook for 2 minutes
12. Return the bacon and onions to the pan and stir cook for 1 minute
13. Serve and enjoy!

68. Pork Stuffed Bell Peppers (Low-Carb)

Preparation Time: 10 minutes/Cooking Time: 25 minutes/Serves: 4 Servings

Nutrition Per Serving: Carbohydrates: 3 grams/Fat: 3 grams/Protein: 10 grams/Fiber: 1 gram/Calories: 140

Ingredients

- 1 teaspoon Cajun spice
- 1 pound pork, ground
- 1 tablespoon tomato paste
- 6 garlic cloves, minced
- 1 yellow onion, chopped
- 4 big bell peppers, tops cut off and deseeded
- Pinch of salt
- Black pepper, as needed

Directions

1. Take a pan and place it over medium-high heat
2. Add oil and let the oil heat up
3. Add garlic, onion and cook for 4 minutes
4. Add meat and gently stir cook for 10 minutes
5. Season with salt and pepper according to your desire
6. Add Cajun seasoning and tomato paste
7. Stir cook for 3 minutes more
8. Stuff bell peppers with the mix and transfer to a pre-heated grill
9. Grill for 3 minutes on each side
10. Divide between plates and serve
11. Enjoy!

69.Caramelized Pork Chops (Low-Carb)

Preparation Time: 5 minutes/Cooking Time: 30 minutes/Serves: 5 Servings

Nutrition Per Serving: Carbohydrates: 4 grams/Fat: 20 grams/Protein: 27 grams/Fiber: 1 gram/Calories: 271

Ingredients

- 4 pounds pork chops
- 4 ounces green chili, chopped
- 2 tablespoons chili powder
- ½ teaspoon dried oregano
- ½ teaspoon ground cumin
- 2 garlic cloves, minced
- Salt, as needed

Directions

1. Rub up the chops with 1 teaspoon of pepper and 2 teaspoons of seasoning salt
2. Take a skillet and heat some oil over medium heat
3. Brown your pork chops on both sides
4. Add water and onions to the pan
5. Cover the skillet and lower the heat; simmer for about 20 minutes
6. Turn your chops over and add the rest of the pepper and salt
7. Cover the skillet and cook until the water evaporates and the onions turn brown with a medium-soft texture
8. Remove the chops from your pan and serve with some onions on top!

70.Italian Pork Chops (Low-Carb)

Preparation Time: 10 minutes/Cooking Time: 40 minutes/Serves: 4 Servings

Nutrition Per Serving: Carbohydrates: 6 grams/Fat: 10 grams/Protein: 19 grams/Fiber: 2 grams/Calories: 210

Ingredients

- 4 pork chops
- 1 tablespoon fresh oregano, chopped
- 2 garlic cloves, peeled and minced
- 1 tablespoon canola oil
- 15 ounces canned tomatoes, diced
- 1 tablespoon tomato paste
- Salt and pepper to taste
- ¼ cup tomato juice

Directions

1. Heat up a pan with oil over medium-high heat
2. Add pork chops, seasoned with salt and pepper
3. Cook for 3 minutes
4. Flip and cook for 3 minutes more
5. Return the pan to medium heat
6. Add garlic and stir cook for 10 seconds
7. Add tomato juice, tomato paste, and tomatoes, bring to a boil, and lower heat to medium-low
8. Add pork chops, stir, and cover pan
9. Simmer for 30 minutes
10. Transfer chops to a platter and add oregano to pan, stir cook for 2 minutes
11. Pour mixture over pork chops
12. Serve and enjoy!

71. Mushroom Pork Chops (Low-Carb)

Preparation Time: 10 minutes/Cooking Time: 40 minutes/Serves: 6 Servings

Nutrition Per Serving: Carbohydrates: 8 grams/Fat: 10 grams/Protein: 30 grams/Fiber: 2 grams/Calories: 600

Ingredients

- 8 ounces mushrooms, sliced
- 1 teaspoon garlic
- 1 onion, peeled and chopped
- 1 cup mayonnaise
- 3 pork chops, boneless
- 1 teaspoon ground nutmeg
- 1 tablespoon balsamic vinegar
- ½ cup coconut oil

Directions

1. Take a pan and place it over medium heat
2. Add oil and let it heat up
3. Add mushrooms and onions; stir
4. Cook for 4 minutes
5. Add pork chops, season with nutmeg and garlic powder; brown both sides
6. Transfer the pan to the oven and bake for 30 minutes at 350 degrees F
7. Transfer pork chops to plates and keep them warm
8. Take a pan and place it over medium heat
9. Add vinegar and mayonnaise over the mushroom mixture and stir for a few minutes
10. Drizzle sauce over pork chops
11. Enjoy!

72. Paprika Lamb Chops (Low-Carb)

Preparation Time: 10 minutes/Cooking Time: 15 minutes/Serves: 2 Servings

Nutrition Per Serving: Carbohydrates: 4 grams/Fat: 5 grams/Protein: 8 grams/Fiber: 1 gram/Calories: 200

Ingredients

- 2 lamb racks, cut into chops
- Salt and pepper to taste
- 3 tablespoons paprika
- ¾ cup cumin powder
- 1 teaspoon chili powder

Directions

1. Take a bowl and add paprika, cumin, chili, salt, and pepper; stir
2. Add lamb chops and rub the mixture over them well
3. Heat grill to medium temperature and add lamb chops; cook for 5 minutes
4. Flip and cook for 5 minutes more, flip again
5. Cook for 2 minutes, flip and cook for 2 minutes more
6. Serve and enjoy!

73. Fennel and Figs Lamb (Low-Carb)

Preparation Time: 5 minutes/Cooking Time: 10 minutes/Serves: 4 Servings

Nutrition Per Serving: Carbohydrates: 5 grams/Fat: 3 grams/Protein: 10 grams/Fiber: 2 grams/Calories: 230

Ingredients

- 12 ounces lamb racks
- 2 fennel bulbs, sliced
- Salt and pepper to taste
- 2 tablespoons olive oil
- 4 figs, cut in half
- 1/8 cup apple cider vinegar
- 1 tablespoon swerve

Directions

1. Take a bowl and add fennel, figs, vinegar, swerve, and oil; toss
2. Transfer to a baking dish
3. Season with salt and pepper
4. Bake for 15 minutes at 400 degrees F
5. Season lamb with salt and pepper and transfer to a heated pan over medium-high heat
6. Cook for a few minutes
7. Add lamb to the baking dish with fennel and bake for 20 minutes
8. Divide between plates and serve
9. Enjoy!

74. Hearty Lamb Salad (Low-Carb)

Preparation Time: 5 minutes/Cooking Time: 35 minutes/Serves: 4 Servings

Nutrition Per Serving: Carbohydrates: 5 grams/Fat: 33 grams/Protein: 7 grams/Fiber: 2 grams/Calories: 334

Ingredients

- 1 tablespoon olive oil
- 3 pounds leg of lamb, bone removed, leg butterflied
- Salt and pepper to taste
- 1 teaspoon cumin
- Pinch of dried thyme
- 2 garlic cloves, peeled and minced

For Salad

- 4 ounces feta cheese, crumbled
- ½ cup pecans
- 2 cups spinach
- 1 and ½ tablespoons lemon juice
- ¼ cup olive oil
- 1 cup fresh mint, chopped

Directions

1. Rub lamb with salt and pepper, 1 tablespoon oil, thyme, cumin, and minced garlic
2. Pre-heat your grill to medium-high and transfer lamb
3. Cook for 40 minutes, making sure to flip the meat once
4. Take a lined baking sheet and spread pecans over it
5. Toast pecans in oven for 10 minutes at 350 degrees F
6. Transfer grilled lamb to a cutting board and let it cool
7. Slice
8. Take a salad bowl and add spinach, 1 cup mint, feta cheese, ¼ cup olive oil, lemon juice, toasted pecans, salt, and pepper; toss well
9. Add lamb slices on top
10. Serve and enjoy!

75. Simple Lamb Chops (Low-Carb)

Preparation Time: 30 minutes/Cooking Time: 5-10 minutes/Serves: 6 Servings

Nutrition Per Serving: Carbohydrates: 2 grams/Fat: 40 grams/Protein: 47 grams/Fiber: 4 grams/Calories: 566

Ingredients

- ¼ cup olive oil
- ¼ cup mint, fresh and chopped
- 8 lamb rib chops
- 1 tablespoon garlic, minced
- 1 tablespoon rosemary, fresh and chopped

Directions

1. Add rosemary, garlic, mint, and olive oil into a bowl and mix well
2. Keep a tablespoon of the mixture on the side for later use
3. Toss lamb chops into the marinade, letting them marinate for 30 minutes
4. Take a cast-iron skillet and place it over medium-high heat
5. Add lamb and cook for 2 minutes per side for medium-rare
6. Let the lamb rest for a few minutes and drizzle the remaining marinade over it
7. Serve and enjoy!

76. South Western Pork Chops (Low-Carb)

Preparation Time: 5 minutes/Cooking Time: 15 minutes/Serves: 4 Servings

Nutrition Per Serving: Carbohydrates: 4 grams/Fat: 4 grams/Protein: 0.5 grams/Fiber: 2 grams/Calories: 184

Ingredients

- Cooking spray, as needed
- 4-ounce pork loin chop, boneless and with fat trimmed
- 1/3 cup salsa
- 2 tablespoons fresh lime juice
- ¼ cup fresh cilantro, chopped

Directions

1. Take a large non-stick skillet and spray it with cooking spray
2. Heat it up until hot over high heat
3. Press the chops with your palm to flatten them slightly
4. Add them to the skillet and cook for 1 minute on each side until they are nicely browned
5. Lower the heat to medium-low
6. Combine the salsa and lime juice
7. Pour the mix over the chops
8. Simmer uncovered for about 8 minutes until the chops are perfectly done
9. If needed, sprinkle some cilantro on top
10. Serve!

77. Smothered Pork Chops (Low-Carb)

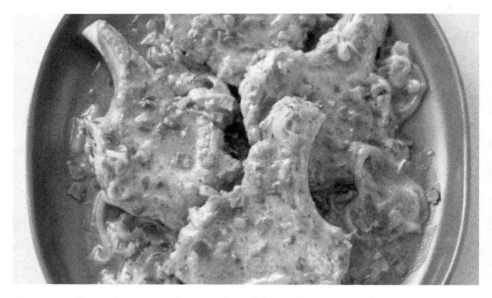

Preparation Time: 5 minutes/Cooking Time: 30 minutes/Serves: 4 Servings

Nutrition Per Serving: Carbohydrates: 1.3 grams/Fat: 10 grams/Protein: 2 grams/Fiber: 2 grams/Calories: 261

Ingredients

- 4 pork chops, bone-in
- 2 tablespoons of olive oil
- ¼ cup of vegetable broth
- ½ pound of sweet potatoes, peeled and chopped
- 1 large onion, sliced
- 2 garlic cloves, minced
- 2 teaspoons of rubbed sage
- 1 teaspoon thyme, ground
- Salt and pepper, as needed

Directions

1. Preheat your oven to 350 degrees Fahrenheit
2. Take a large skillet and place it over medium heat
3. Add a tablespoon of oil and allow the oil to heat up
4. Add pork chops and cook them for 4-5 minutes per side until browned
5. Transfer chops to a baking dish
6. Pour broth over the chops
7. Add remaining oil to the pan and sauté potatoes, onion, and garlic for 3-4 minutes
8. Take a large bowl and add potatoes, garlic, onion, thyme, sage, pepper, and salt
9. Transfer this mixture to the baking dish (with the pork)
10. Bake for 20-30 minutes
11. Serve and enjoy!

78. Skillet Baked Pork Chops and Apple

Preparation Time: 5 minutes/Cooking Time: 25 minutes/Serves: 4 Servings

Nutrition Per Serving: Carbohydrates: 18 grams/Fat: 15 grams/Protein: 88 grams/Fiber: 5 grams/Calories: 579

Ingredients

- 1 teaspoon ground pepper, fresh
- 1 teaspoon sea salt
- 2 tablespoons sage, chopped
- 1 tablespoon Dijon mustard
- ½ cup fresh apple cider
- 2 apples, cored and sliced into 8 pieces
- 1 large onion, halved and sliced into 8 pieces
- 1 large onion, halved and sliced into ¼ inch thick slices
- 1 tablespoon avocado oil
- 4 boneless pork chops, 6 ounces each, trimmed of fat

Directions

1. Preheat your oven to 400 degrees F
2. Pat the pork chops dry with a paper towel and season well with pepper and salt
3. Take a large iron pan and place it over medium-high heat
4. Add pork and sear the chops until both sides are browned; it should take about 2-3 minutes per side
5. Add onions and apples; sauté for about 5 minutes
6. Add apple cider, sage, mustard, salt, and pepper; cook for about 2 minutes until the cider has been reduced to half
7. Return the browned pork chops to the mix and transfer to an oven
8. Cook for about 6-8 minutes at a high temperature until the internal temperature of the pork reaches 154 degrees F
9. Serve and enjoy!

79. Sesame Pork Chops (Low-Carb)

Preparation Time: 5 minutes/Cooking Time: 15 minutes/Serves: 3 Servings

Nutrition Per Serving: Carbohydrates: 8 grams/Fat: 20 grams/Protein: 15 grams/Fiber: 2 grams/Calories: 257

Ingredients

- 1 tablespoon olive oil
- 1 and ½ pounds boneless pork chops

For homemade Sesame Sauce

- 3 cups fresh green beans
- 1 teaspoon sriracha
- 2 teaspoons garlic, minced
- 2 teaspoons ginger, minced
- 3 tablespoons sesame oil
- 1 tablespoon rice vinegar

- 1 tablespoon brown sugar swerve
- ¼ cup gluten-free soy sauce

Directions

1. Take a large skillet and place it over medium heat
2. Add sliced pork chops into the skillet and let them cook for about 3-4 minutes until nicely browned
3. Stir and cook for 3-4 minutes more until the pork is cooked well
4. Take a small measuring cup and add sesame sauce ingredients to the mix and stir well
5. Pour the mixture into the skillet along with the green beans
6. Stir well
7. Bring down the heat to low and cover; cook for about 5 minutes
8. Serve and enjoy!

80. Stir Fry Pork

Preparation Time: 5 minutes/Cooking Time: 15 minutes/Serves: 2 Servings

Nutrition Per Serving: Carbohydrates: 16 grams/Fat: 37 grams/Protein: 16 grams/Fiber: 4 grams/Calories: 433

Ingredients

- 1 head butter lettuce
- ½ cup cilantro, chopped
- ½ cup green scallions, chopped
- 2-3 green chilis, sliced
- 1 tablespoon lemon juice
- 2 teaspoons spicy chili sauce of your choice
- 1 tablespoon gluten-free soy sauce
- 1 tablespoon garlic, minced
- 1 tablespoon ginger, minced
- 2 tablespoons sesame oil

- 1 tablespoon olive oil
- 1 pound ground pork

Directions

1. Take a 10-inch pan and place it over medium heat
2. Add oil and let the pan heat up. Add ginger and garlic; let sizzle for a few seconds
3. Add ground pork, mix to break up the lumps, and brown the meat, making sure that it is cooked well
4. Chop green onions and cilantro and add them to a bowl on the side
5. After about 8 minutes, the pork should be almost done; push the meat to the side of the pan and add your sliced green and red chilis
6. Add soy sauce, chili sauce, and sesame oil; gently stir
7. Remove from heat and stir everything well
8. Let it sit uncovered for about 3-4 minutes
9. Stir in green onion and cilantro
10. Sprinkle a bit of lemon juice over and stir well
11. Separate the leaves of butter lettuce and serve the dish over lettuce
12. Enjoy!

81. Spicy Pork Chop (Low-Carb)

Preparation Time: 10 minutes + marinate time/Cooking Time: 15 minutes/Serves: 4 Servings

Nutrition Per Serving: Carbohydrates: 3 grams/Fat: 8 grams/Protein: 26 grams/Fiber: 1 gram/Calories: 200

Ingredients

- ¼ cup lime juice
- 4 pork rib chops
- 1 tablespoon coconut oil, melted
- 2 garlic cloves, peeled and minced
- 1 tablespoon chili powder
- 1 teaspoon ground cinnamon
- 2 teaspoons cumin
- Salt and pepper to taste
- ½ teaspoon hot pepper sauce
- Mango, sliced

Directions

1. Take a bowl and mix in lime juice, oil, garlic, cumin, cinnamon, chili powder, salt, pepper, and hot pepper sauce
2. Whisk well
3. Add pork chops and toss
4. Let it refrigerate for 4 hours
5. Pre-heat your grill to medium and transfer pork chops to a pre-heated grill
6. Grill for 7 minutes, flip, and cook for 7 minutes more
7. Divide between serving platters and serve with mango slices
8. Enjoy!

Chapter 12: Fish and Seafood

82. Walnut Encrusted Salmon (Low-Carb)

Preparation Time: 5 minutes/Cooking Time: 15 minutes/Serves: 2 Servings

Nutrition Per Serving: Carbohydrates: 4 grams/Fat: 43 grams/Protein: 20 grams/Fiber: 2 grams/Calories: 373

Ingredients

- ½ cup walnuts
- 2 tablespoons stevia
- ½ tablespoon Dijon mustard
- ¼ teaspoon dill
- 2 salmon fillets (3 ounces each)
- 1 tablespoon olive oil
- Salt and pepper to taste

Directions

1. Preheat your oven to 350 degrees F
2. Add walnuts, mustard, stevia to a food processor and process until the desired consistency is achieved
3. Take a frying pan and place it over medium heat
4. Add oil and let it heat up
5. Add salmon and sear for 3 minutes
6. Add walnut mix and coat well
7. Transfer coated salmon to the baking sheet, bake in the oven for 8 minutes
8. Serve and enjoy!

83. Awesome Glazed Salmon (Low-Carb)

Preparation Time: 10-15 minutes/Cooking Time: 10 minutes/Serves: 4 Servings

Nutrition Per Serving: Carbohydrates: 3 grams/Fat: 24 grams/Protein: 35 grams/Fiber: 1 gram/Calories: 372

Ingredients

- 4 pieces salmon fillets, 5 ounces each
- 4 tablespoons coconut aminos
- 4 teaspoons olive oil
- 2 teaspoons ginger, minced
- 4 teaspoons garlic, minced
- 2 tablespoons sugar-free ketchup
- 4 tablespoons dry white wine
- 2 tablespoons red boat fish sauce

Directions

1. Take a bowl and mix in coconut aminos, garlic, ginger, and fish sauce; mix
2. Add salmon and let it marinate for 15-20 minutes
3. Take a skillet/pan and place it over medium heat
4. Add oil and let it heat up
5. Add salmon fillets and cook on HIGH for 3-4 minutes per side
6. Remove to a dish once the fish is crispy
7. Add sauce and wine to the pan
8. Simmer for 5 minutes on low heat
9. Return salmon to the glaze and flip until both sides are glazed
10. Serve and enjoy!

84. Baked Orange Juice Salmon (Low-Carb)

Preparation Time: 5 minutes/Cooking Time: 10 minutes/Serves: 2 Servings

Nutrition Per Serving: Carbohydrates: 1 gram/Fat: 3 grams/Protein: 7 grams/Fiber: 0.1 gram/Calories: 300

Ingredients

- ½ pound salmon steak
- Juice of 1 orange
- Pinch each of ginger powder, black pepper, and salt
- Juice of ½ lemon
- 1 ounce of coconut milk

Directions

1. Rub salmon steak with spices and let it sit for 15 minutes
2. Take a bowl and squeeze the orange
3. Squeeze lemon juice as well and mix with the orange
4. Pour milk into the mixture and stir
5. Take a baking dish and line it with aluminum foil
6. Place steak on it and pour the sauce over the steak
7. Cover with another sheet of foil and bake for 10 minutes at 350 degrees F
8. Serve and enjoy!

85. Broccoli and Tilapia Dish (Low-Carb)

Preparation Time: 5 minutes/Cooking Time: 14 minutes/Serves: 4 Servings

Nutrition Per Serving: Carbohydrates: 2 grams/Fat: 25 grams/Protein: 29 grams/Fiber: 1 gram/Calories: 362

Ingredients

- 6 ounce of tilapia, frozen
- 1 tablespoon of butter
- 1 tablespoon of garlic, minced
- 1 teaspoon of lemon pepper seasoning
- 1 cup of broccoli florets, fresh

Directions

1. Preheat your oven to 350 degrees Fahrenheit
2. Put fish into aluminum foil packets
3. Arrange broccoli around the fish
4. Sprinkle lemon pepper on top
5. Close the foil packets and seal
6. Bake for 14 minutes
7. Take a bowl and add garlic and butter, mix well, and set the mixture off to the side
8. Remove the packets from the oven and transfer them to a platter
9. Place butter on top of the fish and broccoli, serve, and enjoy!

86. Baked Halibut

Preparation Time: 5 minutes/Cooking Time: 30 minutes/Serves: 4 Servings

Nutrition Per Serving: Carbohydrates: 10 grams/Fat: 26 grams/Protein: 36 grams/Fiber: 2 grams/Calories: 429

Ingredients

- 6 ounces halibut fillets
- 1 tablespoon Greek seasoning
- 1 large tomato, chopped
- 1 onion, chopped
- 5 ounces kalamata olives, pitted
- ¼ cup capers
- ¼ cup olive oil
- 1 tablespoon lemon juice
- Salt and pepper, as needed

Directions

1. Preheat your oven to 350 degrees Fahrenheit
2. Transfer the halibut fillets onto a large aluminum foil
3. Season with Greek seasoning
4. Take a bowl and add tomato, onion, olives, olive oil, capers, pepper, lemon juice, and salt
5. Mix well and spoon the tomato mix over the halibut
6. Seal the edges of the foil and fold to make a packet
7. Place the packet on a baking sheet and bake in your oven for 30-40 minutes
8. Serve once the fish flakes off and enjoy!
9. Serve over rice cauliflower, if desired

87. Garlic and Parsley Scallops (Low-Carb)

Preparation Time: 5 minutes/Cooking Time: 25 minutes/Serves: 6 Servings

Nutrition Per Serving: Carbohydrates: 5 grams/Fat: 31 grams/Protein: 29 grams/Fiber: 1 gram/Calories: 417

Ingredients

- 8 tablespoons butter
- 2 garlic cloves, minced
- 16 large sea scallops
- Salt and pepper to taste
- 1 and ½ tablespoons olive oil

Directions

1. Season scallops with salt and pepper
2. Take a skillet and place it over medium heat, add oil, and let it heat up
3. Sauté scallops for 2 minutes per side; repeat until all scallops are cooked
4. Add butter to the skillet and let it melt
5. Stir in garlic and cook for 15 minutes
6. Return scallops to skillet and stir to coat
7. Serve and enjoy!

88. Coconut and Hazelnut Haddock (Low-Carb)

Preparation Time: 5 minutes/Cooking Time: 12 minutes/Serves: 4 Servings

Nutrition Per Serving: Carbohydrates: 1 gram/Fat: 24 grams/Protein: 20 grams/Fiber: 0.1 gram/Calories: 299

Ingredients

- 4 haddock fillets (5 ounces each), boneless
- 2 tablespoons coconut oil, melted
- 1 cup coconut, shredded and unsweetened
- ¼ cup hazelnuts, ground
- Salt to taste
- Some cooked spinach

Directions

1. Preheat your oven to 400 degrees F
2. Line a baking sheet with parchment paper
3. Keep it on the side
4. Pat fish fillets with a paper towel and season with salt
5. Take a bowl and stir in hazelnuts and shredded coconut
6. Drag fish fillets through the coconut mix until both sides are coated well
7. Transfer to a baking dish
8. Brush with coconut oil
9. Bake for about 12 minutes until flaky
10. Serve over a bed of cooked spinach and enjoy!

89. Italian Salmon Platter (Low-Carb)

Preparation Time: 5 minutes/Cooking Time: 6 minutes/Serves: 3 Servings

Nutrition Per Serving: Carbohydrates: 3 grams/Fat: 34 grams/Protein: 15 grams/Fiber: 1 gram/Calories: 464

Ingredients

- ¾ cup of water
- A few sprigs of parsley, basil, tarragon, basil
- 1 pound of salmon, skin on
- 3 teaspoons of ghee
- ¼ teaspoon of salt
- ½ teaspoon of pepper
- ½ of lemon, thinly sliced
- 1 whole carrot, julienned

Directions

1. Set your pot to sauté mode and put in water and herbs
2. Place a steamer rack inside your pot and place in salmon
3. Drizzle ghee on top of the salmon and season with salt and pepper
4. Cover with lemon slices
5. Lock the lid and cook on HIGH pressure for 3 minutes
6. Release the pressure naturally over 10 minutes
7. Transfer the salmon to a serving platter
8. Set your pot to sauté mode and add vegetables
9. Cook for 1-2 minutes
10. Serve vegetables with the salmon
11. Enjoy!

90.Feisty Grilled Lime Shrimp (Low-Carb)

Preparation Time: 10-20 minutes/Cooking Time: 5 minutes/Serves: 3 Servings

Nutrition Per Serving: Carbohydrates: 1.2 grams/Fat: 3 grams/Protein: 13 grams/Fiber: 0.1 gram/Calories: 188

Ingredients

- 1 pound medium shrimp, peeled and deveined
- 1 lime, juiced
- ½ cup olive oil
- 3 tablespoons Cajun seasoning

Directions

1. Take a re-sealable zip bag and add lime juice, Cajun seasoning, and olive oil
2. Add shrimp and shake it well; let it marinate for 20 minutes
3. Preheat your outdoor grill to medium heat
4. Lightly grease the grate
5. Remove shrimp from marinade and cook for 2 minutes per side
6. Serve and enjoy!

91. Exciting Calamari

Preparation Time: 10 minutes + Marinate Time/Cooking Time: 8 minutes/Serves: 3 Servings

Nutrition Per Serving: Carbohydrates: 12 grams/Fat: 13 grams/Protein: 3 grams/Fiber: 4 grams/Calories: 159

Ingredients

- 2 tablespoons extra virgin olive oil
- 1 teaspoon chili powder
- ½ teaspoon ground cumin
- Zest of 1 lime
- Juice of 1 lime
- Dash of sea salt
- 1 and ½ pounds squid, cleaned and split open, with tentacles cut into ½-inch rounds
- 2 tablespoons cilantro, chopped
- 2 tablespoons red bell pepper, minced

Directions

1. Take a medium bowl and stir in olive oil, chili powder, cumin, lime zest, sea salt, lime juice, and pepper
2. Add squid and let it marinade. Stir to coat and let it refrigerate for 1 hour
3. Pre-heat your oven to broil
4. Arrange squid on a baking sheet, broil for 8 minutes; turn once and broil until tender
5. Garnish the broiled calamari with cilantro and red bell pepper
6. Serve and enjoy!

Chapter 13: Snacks and Appetizers

92. Cool Warm Green Beans Dish (Low-Carb|Vegan)

Preparation Time: 5 minutes/Cooking Time: 12 minutes/Serves: 4 Servings

Nutrition Per Serving: Carbohydrates: 4 grams/Fat: 8 grams/Protein: 2 grams/Fiber: 2 grams/Calories: 93

Ingredients

- 2 garlic cloves, minced
- Red pepper flakes to taste
- Salt to taste
- 2 tablespoons Vegan butter
- 4 cups green beans, trimmed

Directions

1. Bring a pot of salted water to boil
2. Once the water starts to boil, add beans and cook for 3 minutes
3. Take a bowl of ice water and drain beans, plunge them into the ice water
4. Once cooled, set them aside
5. Take a medium skillet and place it over medium heat; add ghee and melt
6. Add red pepper, salt, and garlic
7. Cook for 1 minute
8. Add beans and toss until coated well, cook for 3 minutes
9. Serve and enjoy!

93. Lemon Broccoli Roast (Low-Carb|Vegan)

Preparation Time: 10 minutes/Cooking Time: 15 minutes/Serves: 2 Servings

Nutrition Per Serving: Carbohydrates: 4 grams/Fat: 2 grams/Protein: 3 grams/Fiber: 2 grams/Calories: 49

Ingredients

- 2 heads of broccoli, separated into florets
- 2 teaspoons extra virgin olive oil
- 1 teaspoon salt
- ½ teaspoon pepper
- 1 garlic clove, minced
- ½ teaspoon lemon juice

Directions

1. Pre-heat your oven to a temperature of 400 degrees F
2. Take a large bowl and add broccoli florets with some extra virgin olive oil, pepper, sea salt, and garlic
3. Spread the broccoli out in a single even layer on a fine baking sheet
4. Bake in your pre-heated oven for about 15-20 minutes until the florets are soft enough so that they can be pierced with a fork
5. Squeeze lemon juice over them generously before serving
6. Enjoy!

94. Cool Avocado Chips (Low-Carb|Vegan)

Preparation Time: 5 minutes/Cooking Time: 30 minutes/Serves: 3 Servings

Nutrition Per Serving: Carbohydrates: 4 grams/Fat: 10 grams/Protein: 7 grams/Fiber: 1 gram/Calories: 120

Ingredients

- Fresh black pepper
- Salt, as needed
- ½ teaspoon Italian seasoning
- ½ teaspoon garlic powder
- 1 teaspoon lemon juice
- 1 large ripe avocado
- ¾ cup coconut cream

Directions

1. Preheat your oven to 325 degrees F
2. Take two baking sheets and line them with parchment paper
3. Take a medium-sized bowl and add avocado; mash it with a fork until you have a smooth mixture
4. Stir in coconut cream, garlic powder, lemon juice, and seasoning
5. Season more with salt and pepper
6. Place about a heaping teaspoon scoop of the mix on your baking sheet, making sure to leave about a 3-inch distance between each scoop
7. Flatten them to a 3-inch width
8. Bake for about 30 minutes until crispy
9. Serve and enjoy!

95. Exotic Cucumber Sushi (Low-Carb|Vegan)

Preparation Time: 10 minutes/Cooking Time: Nil/Serves: 2 Servings

Nutrition Per Serving: Carbohydrates: 9 grams/Fat: 16 grams/Protein: 1 gram/Fiber: 2 grams/Calories: 190

Ingredients

For Sushi

- 2 small carrots, thinly sliced
- ½ yellow bell pepper, thinly sliced
- ½ red bell pepper, thinly sliced
- ¼ avocado, sliced
- 2 medium cucumbers, halved

For Sauce

- 1 teaspoon soy sauce
- 1 tablespoon sriracha
- 1/3 cup coconut cream

Directions

1. Take a small spoon, remove the seeds from the center of the cucumber, and hollow them out
2. Press avocado into the center of your cucumber using a butter knife
3. Slide in the sliced bell pepper and carrots until the cucumber shell is full of your vegetables
4. Take a small bowl and add cream, soy sauce, and sriracha; whisk well
5. Slice the cucumber into 1-inch rounds and serve with the sauce

96. Roasted Herb Crackers (Low-Carb|Vegan)

Preparation Time: 5 minutes/Cooking Time: 120 minutes/Serves: 75 crackers

Nutrition Per Serving: Carbohydrates: 1 gram/Fat: 5 grams/Protein: 1.3 grams/Fiber: 4 grams/Calories: 34

Ingredients

- ¼ cup avocado oil
- 10 celery sticks
- 1 sprig fresh rosemary, stem discarded
- 2 sprigs fresh thyme, stems discarded
- 2 tablespoons apple cider vinegar
- 1 teaspoon Himalayan salt
- 3 cups ground flax seeds

Directions

1. Preheat your oven to 225 degrees F
2. Line a baking sheet with parchment paper and set it aside
3. Add oil, herbs, celery, vinegar, and salt to a food processor and pulse until you have an even mixture
4. Add flax and puree
5. Let it sit for 2-3 minutes
6. Transfer batter to your prepared baking sheet and spread evenly, cut into cracker shapes
7. Bake for 60 minutes, flip, and bake for 60 minutes more
8. Enjoy!

97. Onion and Thyme Crackers (Low-Carb|Vegan)

Preparation Time: 5 minutes/Cooking Time: 120 minutes/Serves: 75 crackers

Nutrition Per Serving: Carbohydrates: 0.3 gram/Fat: 2.7 grams/Protein: 0.4 gram/Fiber: 0.1 gram/Calories: 18

Ingredients

- 1 garlic clove, minced
- 1 cup sweet onion, coarsely chopped
- 2 teaspoons fresh thyme leaves
- ¼ cup avocado oil
- ¼ teaspoon Himalayan salt
- Freshly ground black pepper
- ¼ cup sunflower seeds
- 1 and ½ cups roughly ground flax seeds

Directions

1. Preheat your oven to 225 degrees F
2. Line two baking sheets with parchment paper and keep it on the side
3. Add garlic, onion, thyme, oil, salt, and pepper to a food processor
4. Add sunflower and flax seeds; pulse until pureed
5. Transfer batter to prepared baking sheets and spread evenly; cut into crackers
6. Bake for 60 minutes
7. Remove parchment paper and flip crackers; bake for another hour
8. If crackers are thick, it will take more time
9. Remove from oven and let them cool
10. Enjoy!

98. Awesome Cacao Nut Truffles

Preparation Time: 10 minutes + 60 minutes chill time/Cooking Time: Nil/Serves: 16 truffles

Nutrition Per Serving: Carbohydrates: 7 grams/Fat: 12 grams/Protein: 5 grams/Fiber: 1 grams/Calories:148

Ingredients

- ¼ teaspoon cinnamon, ground
- 2 tablespoons raw honey
- 3 tablespoons coconut oil, melted
- ¼ cup cacao, raw and powdered
- ½ cup creamy almont butter, unsalted
- 1 and ½ cups raw almonds
- Additional shredded coconuts

Directions

1. Take your food processor and add almonds, pulse them until finely ground
2. Add rest of the ingredients to the food processor and pulse until you have a smooth dough with a sticky texture, it should take about 1-2 minutes
3. Scoop about 1 heaping tablespoon of dough at a time and form balls of 1 and ½ inch size. Roll the balls in shredded coconut if desired
4. Transfer the balls to an aluminum foil/parchment paper lined baking sheet
5. Let them chill in your fridge for 60 minutes
6. Serve and enjoy once ready!

99. Walnuts and Asparagus Combo (Low-Carb|Vegan)

Preparation Time: 5 minutes/Cooking Time: 5 minutes/Serves: 2 Servings

Nutrition Per Serving: Carbohydrates: 2 grams/Fat: 12 grams/Protein: 3 grams/Fiber: 2 grams/Calories: 124

Ingredients

- 1 and ½ tablespoons olive oil
- ¾ pound asparagus, trimmed
- ¼ cup walnuts, chopped
- Salt and pepper to taste

Directions

1. Place a skillet over medium heat, add olive oil and let it heat up
2. Add asparagus, sauté for 5 minutes until browned
3. Season with salt and pepper
4. Remove from heat
5. Add walnuts and toss
6. Serve warm!

100. Garlic Lemon Soup (Low-Carb|Vegan)

Preparation Time: 5 minutes/Cooking Time: 10 minutes/Serves: 2 Servings

Nutrition Per Serving: Carbohydrates: 6 grams/Fat: 7 grams/Protein: 3 grams/Fiber: 4 grams/Calories: 100

Ingredients

- 1 avocado, pitted and chopped
- 1 cucumber, chopped
- 2 bunches spinach
- 1 and ½ cups watermelon, chopped
- 1 bunch cilantro, roughly chopped
- Juice from 2 lemons
- ½ cup coconut aminos
- ½ cup lime juice

Directions

1. Add cucumber and avocado to your blender and pulse well
2. Add cilantro, spinach, and watermelon; blend
3. Add lemon, lime juice, and coconut amino
4. Pulse a few more times
5. Transfer to a soup bowl and enjoy!

101. Pumpkin Spicy Chili Dish

Preparation Time: 5 minutes/Cooking Time: 25 minutes/Serves: 2 Servings

Nutrition Per Serving: Carbohydrates: 14 grams/Fat: 16 grams/Protein: 27 grams/Fiber: 4 grams/Calories: 312

Ingredients

- 3 cups yellow onion, chopped
- 8 garlic cloves, chopped
- 1 pound turkey, ground
- 2 cans (15 ounces each) fire-roasted tomatoes
- 2 cups pumpkin puree
- 1 cup chicken broth
- 4 teaspoons chili spice
- 1 teaspoon ground cinnamon
- 1 teaspoon sea salt

Directions

1. Take a large pot and place it over medium-high heat
2. Add coconut oil and let it heat up
3. Add onion and garlic; sauté for 5 minutes
4. Add ground turkey and break it up as it cooks; cook for 5 minutes
5. Add remaining ingredients and bring the mix to simmer
6. Simmer for 15 minutes over low heat (lid off)
7. Serve with desired salad
8. Enjoy!

Leave a 1-Click Review!

I would be incredibly thankful if you could take just 60 seconds to write a brief review on Amazon, even if it's just a few sentences!

>> Scan with your camera to leave a quick review:

Thank you and I can't wait to see your thoughts.

Conclusion

The Pegan Diet, introduced by Dr. Mark Hyman, is still a comparatively new dietary program, and people are just slowly beginning to understand its concept and grasp the underlying ideologies and health benefits it offers.

As more time passes, I am pretty sure that this incredible diet will slowly build up an even bigger community all over the globe—where people will collaborate, interact, and inspire each other to bring out their best selves.

Thank you for downloading and reading this book through to the end; I really hope that you found the information within it helpful. I tried my very best to put everything in a very simple and easy-to-understand manner so that anyone can just pick up the book and dive right into the fundamentals of the Pegan Diet.

As with all progressive ideas, there is much more to know about the Pegan Diet than just the information that is found here. This book is designed to act as an entry point for absolute beginners; from here on out, I encourage you to explore more and know more about the diet.

With your fundamentals polished up, you will be able to grasp and implement new concepts of Pegan in your life with absolute ease.

Stay safe, and may you live a long and happy Pegan life.

SPECIAL BONUS!

Want This Bonus book for FREE?

Get **FREE** unlimited access to it and all of my new books by joining the Fan Base!

SCAN W/ YOUR CAMERA TO JOIN!

CPSIA information can be obtained
at www.ICGtesting.com
Printed in the USA
LVHW091923310521
688960LV00001B/11